AN INDIGENOUS VOICE TO PARLIAMENT

Considering a constitutional bridge

AN
INDIGENOUS
VOICE TO PARLIAMENT

Considering a constitutional bridge

Frank Brennan

garratt
PUBLISHING

garratt PUBLISHING

Published in Australia by
Garratt Publishing
32 Glenvale Crescent
Mulgrave, VIC 3170
www.garrattpublishing.com.au

Cover Design by Guy Holt Design
Text Design by Mike Kuszla
Edited by Greg Hill
Cover image © Frank Brennan

Printed by Advent Printing

ISBN 9781922484659

A catalogue record for this book is available from the National Library of Australia

Cataloguing in Publication information for this title is available from the National Library of Australia.
www.nla.gov.au

The authors and publisher gratefully acknowledge the permission granted to reproduce the copyright material in this book. Every effort has been made to trace copyright holders and to obtain their permission for the use of copyright material.

The publisher apologises for any errors or omissions in the above list and would be grateful if notified of any corrections that should be incorporated in future reprints or editions of this book.

Dedicated to my late father, Gerard,
who cared passionately and thought carefully
about the legal recognition of the entitlements of
Aboriginal and Torres Strait Islander peoples

Frank Brennan is a Catholic priest, a lawyer and a member of the Jesuit Order. He has been a long-time advocate of Aboriginal and Torres Strait Islander People rights, having commenced this public ministry as Adviser to the Queensland Catholic Bishops in 1982. He was made an Officer of the Order of Australia in 1995 for services to Aboriginal Australians, particularly as an advocate in the areas of law, social justice and reconciliation. He and Senator Patrick Dodson shared the inaugural Human Rights Award from the Australian Council for Overseas Aid. In 2015, he published *No Small Change: The Road to Recognition for Indigenous Australia.* He chaired the National Human Rights Consultation for the Rudd Government, was a member of the expert panel on religious freedom for the Turnbull Government, and a member of the Morrison Government's Senior Advisory Group guiding the co-design process to develop an Aboriginal and Torres Strait Islander Voice.

CONTENTS

Prologue

Where I'm Coming From 1

Chapter 1

A Task for Every Conscientious Citizen 11

Chapter 2

The Australian Constitution and Earlier Amendments 19

Chapter 3

History of Proposals for Indigenous Recognition 29
2007–2017

Chapter 4

The *Uluru Statement* and the Referendum Council 2017 45

Chapter 5

Mr Albanese at Garma 2022 61

Chapter 6

Seeking a Way Forward 71

Chapter 7

The 'Yes' Case 83

Chapter 8

The 'No' Case 95

Chapter 9

Where to from here?   109

Appendix

Uluru Statement from the Heart   119

PROLOGUE
Where I'm Coming From

Appearing at the Garma Festival on 30 July 2022, Prime Minister Anthony Albanese announced: 'I would like us to present the Australian people with the clearest possible referendum question. We should consider asking our fellow Australians something as simple, but something as clear, as this: do you support an alteration to the Constitution that establishes an Aboriginal and Torres Strait *Islander Voice?*'

The Prime Minister described this as, 'A straightforward proposition. A simple principle. A question from the heart.' My hope is that by the end of 2023, when Australians are asked that question, the majority will answer 'Yes'. But at the moment I don't see it as a straightforward proposition. The simple principle has been overlaid with complexities.

The head requires some answers before the heart can respond. Is the *Voice* to be a *Voice to Parliament* or a *Voice to Parliament and to Government?* Is the Voice to be primarily concerned with special laws applying specifically to Aboriginals and Torres Strait Islanders? Or is the Voice to be able to make representations on all manner of things, including laws and policies which impact both on Aboriginal people and Torres Strait Islanders and also on non-Indigenous Australians? If so, is there any law or policy that does not impact on Aboriginal people and Torres Strait Islanders? Can we design a Voice which will help Aboriginal people and Torres

1

Strait Islanders to live more fulfilling lives without clogging the courts or gluing up the system of government? Many voters will want answers to these questions before being able to answer the simple, clear question on the ballot paper.

My commitment to Aboriginal rights commenced when I was a first-year law student at the University of Queensland in 1971. That's when the first land rights case failed in the Northern Territory Supreme Court. The last all-white Springbok rugby tour came to Australia that year. In my then home state of Queensland, the premier Sir Joh Bjelke Petersen declared a state of emergency so the rugby game could proceed without disruption by protesters agitating against racial discrimination. Young Indigenous activists, including Marcia Langton, spoke about land rights and self-determination at lunchtime forums on campus.

By 1982, I had been appointed an adviser to the Queensland Catholic bishops on Aboriginal affairs. That was the year of the Commonwealth Games in Brisbane. It was known that there would be large protests against the Bjelke Petersen government regarding their policies relating to Aboriginal and Torres Strait Islander peoples in Queensland, particularly regarding Aboriginal reserves where there was no recognition of land rights or of the Aboriginal entitlement to self-management or self-determination.

For the last 40 years, I have attempted to contribute to the Aboriginal struggle for land rights and self-determination. I was involved in the public debates and parliamentary negotiations following upon the High Court decisions in *Mabo* in 1992 and *Wik* in 1996.

In recent years, there has been an increasing focus on the need for constitutional recognition of Aboriginals and Torres Strait

Islanders. In 2015, I published my book *No Small Change* in which I proposed two significant changes to the Australian Constitution.[1] I suggested that the Constitution should commence with an acknowledgment of the First Australians in these terms:

- We, the people of Australia, recognise that the continent and the islands of Australia were first occupied by Aboriginal and Torres Strait Islander peoples.
- We acknowledge the continuing relationship of Aboriginal and Torres Strait Islander peoples with their traditional lands and waters.
- We acknowledge and respect the continuing cultures, languages, and heritage of Aboriginal and Torres Strait Islander peoples.

I also proposed that the Constitution should provide that the Australian Parliament has power to make laws with respect to the cultures, languages and heritage of the Aboriginal and Torres Strait Islander peoples and their continuing relationship with their traditional lands and waters.

I was taken aback when the book was condemned outright by Aboriginal intellectual leaders Noel Pearson and Marcia Langton. I had come to know Marcia well when she headed up Queensland Premier Wayne Goss's Aboriginal Affairs department. Noel was a young graduate around the traps when I was legal adviser to the Queensland Aboriginal Co-ordinating Council. We had all known each other for decades. We had all been schooled in Joh Bjelke Petersen's Queensland.

---

1   Frank Brennan, *No Small Change: The Road to Recognition for Indigenous Australia*, University of Queensland Press, 2015.

Some two years before the Uluru Statement was penned, Marcia urged Australians to reject my suggested amendments labelling them as 'dismissive and disrespectful of decades of Indigenous advocacy for serious constitutional reform'.[2] Some months before the publication of my book, Noel Pearson had floated the idea of an Indigenous Voice to Parliament. I had said that if such an entity were to be placed in the Constitution, it would be desirable that it first be legislated and road tested so that the voters would have some idea of what they were voting to entrench in the Constitution. Marcia backed Noel's proposal without the need for any preliminary legislated road testing and observed on 2 June 2015:

Brennan calls himself an advocate for Indigenous rights, yet he supports no substantive reform. He suggests that the Indigenous body should be road-tested before our people should be trusted with a body of constitutional status. He also suggests there will be identity issues in deciding who is Indigenous or not, which the High Court would need to resolve. Brennan is wrong. We know who we are. There are established legislative tests which provide rules in relation to Indigenous identity. Finally, the whole point of Pearson's proposal is for a constitutional guarantee that the Indigenous voice is heard in Indigenous affairs. A legislative guarantee will not do. I implore Australians to listen to what Indigenous people want. Not Frank Brennan.

---

2   Michael Gordon, 'Academic Marcia Langton blasts Frank Brennan's recognition plan', *Sydney Morning Herald*, 3 June 2015, available at https://www.smh.com.au/national/academic-marcia-langton-blasts-frank-brennans-recognition-plan-20150602-ghf5pq.html

Noel Pearson then explained his proposal to the public on the ABC *Q&A* on 15 June 2015:

> The substantive provision that I champion with the support of constitutional conservatives is actually a body in the Constitution that would enable Indigenous people to have a voice to the parliament, to provide advice and the views of Indigenous Australians. This is an extremely important idea and it would have great practical benefit to Indigenous Australians in dealing with the executive government of Australia and the Parliament. So, in fact, we are in a situation where constitutional conservatives actually, in being cautious about putting words into the preamble of the Constitution, actually then support Indigenous Australians being represented in a body under the Constitution that would have this role of advising parliament when it makes laws about us. So my position is that symbolism is not enough. There has got to be real practical benefits – real practical democratic benefit – that must flow from recognition. Ancient Australia needs to have a voice in this parliament, to this parliament.[3]

On 3 July 2015, Noel followed up with criticism of me for proposing what he labelled as minimal symbolic change to the Constitution: 'This is not black robe territory two centuries ago. Indigenous people are a polity. We don't need a priest or any other

---

3   ABC, *Q&A*, 15 June 2015, available at https://www.abc.net.au/qanda/magna-carta-magna-qanda/10654792

person to speak on our behalf. This is about a political settlement.'[4] Noel and Marcia wanted to clear the decks of all alternatives for constitutional change. For them, there was only one option: the Voice to Parliament. This was two years before the *Uluru Statement from the Heart*.

In response, I said that I would accept the judgment of Indigenous leaders if it was their view that symbolic change was no better than no change. I said to the respected Fairfax journalist Michael Gordon: 'I have great equanimity on this. I am a non-Indigenous Australian who cares passionately that [Aboriginal people] end up with a better deal under the Constitution, but I am such a believer in self-determination that, of course, it's their call.' That remains my position eight years on.

I happily served as a member of the Morrison government's Senior Advisory Group on the Co-Design of the Voice. That group was led by Marcia, and Noel was a member. The Indigenous community (led largely by Noel and Marcia, together with Pat Anderson and Megan Davis) has now decided to agree to only one form of constitutional recognition – a Voice placed in the Constitution without the need for previous legislation and road testing. They have gone two steps further in recent years, insisting that the Voice be not only a Voice to Parliament but also a Voice to executive government, and that the Voice have the constitutional entitlement to make representations not only on laws specific to Indigenous Australians but also on any 'matters relating to

---

4   Michael Gordon, 'Noel Pearson slams advocate for "modest" Indigenous recognition', *Sydney Morning Herald*, 3 July 2015, available https://www.smh.com.au/politics/federal/noel-pearson-slams-advocate-for-modest-indigenous-recognition-20150703-gi4pu2.html. When speaking of 'black robe territory', Pearson was presumably referring to the seventeenth century Jesuit missionaries who went to the Huron and Iroquois Peoples.

Aboriginal and Torres Strait Islander Peoples'. A Voice extended to executive government could make representations not just to parliament but also to ministers and to public servants.

Nineteen seventy-one was not just the year of my introduction to Aboriginal issues. It was not just the year of the first land rights case. It was the year that Neville Bonner became the first Aboriginal Australian to be sworn in as a member of the Australian parliament. When he delivered his first speech to the Senate he said:

> Mr President, I crave your indulgence and the indulgence of honourable senators in that for a very short time all within me that is Aboriginal yearns to be heard as the voice of the Indigenous people of Australia. For far too long we have been crying out and far too few have heard us. I stand humbly in the presence of honourable senators to bring to their attention what I believe to be the lot of those of my race in 1971. It would be an understatement to say that the lot of fellow Aborigines [*sic*] is not a particularly happy one. We bear emotional scars – the young no less than the older.[5]

Senator Bonner went on to add:

> I want to emphasise the urgency of greater Aboriginal participation particularly in the areas of social development and vocational and general education. I believe there is need for a programme wherein Aborigines [*sic*], and not necessarily academically qualified or young Aborigines [*sic*], but armed with understanding and compassion plus

---

5   Senate, *Hansard*, 8 September 1971, p. 554.

the ability to communicate, can be fielded to liaise with Aborigines and all relevant government departments and organisations working in the field today.'[6]

On 12 March 1974, when responding to The Queen's Speech, Bonner told the Senate:

Mr Deputy President, I felt that I should say the things that I have said because this is the first time that the voice of the Aboriginal people has been heard in this chamber. I realise that I have responsibilities to all sections of the Australian community, but I feel also that I have a particular responsibility to people of my own race.[7]

On 1 July 1974, Neville Bonner introduced this motion to the Senate:

That the Senate accepts the fact that the Indigenous people of Australia, now known as Aborigines [sic] and Torres Strait Islanders, were in possession of this entire nation prior to the 1788 First Fleet landing at Botany Bay, urges the Australian Government to admit prior ownership by the said Indigenous people, and introduce legislation to compensate the people now known as Aborigines [sic] and Torres Strait Islanders for dispossession of their land.

On 19 September 1974, Ministers in the Labor Government

---

6   Ibid.
7   Senate, *Hansard*, 12 March 1974, p. 197.

attempted to thwart all debate on the motion, pleading that the matter was before the courts and therefore not to be discussed (*sub judice*).[8] Later Senator Bonner described the debate as 'reasonable and healthy', with the motion being accepted without dissent.

I was privileged to be in the Senate public gallery on the night of 7 December 1976 when the Senate was debating the *Aboriginal Land Rights Bill*. The great Professor William Edward Hanley Stanner was there. Next day in the Senate, Senator Bonner paid due acknowledgment to Professor Stanner and told the Senate:

> I, as the lone Aboriginal voice in this Parliament, together with my colleagues – men like Fred Chaney, Peter Baume, Alan Missen and quite a few others who have shown a great concern in regard to this Bill and who will be supporting me – will be watching very closely the implementation of this land rights Bill to ensure that my people are not deprived of that to which they are rightly and justly entitled.[9]

On 17 March 1982, Senator Bonner when speaking up for the rights of the Aboriginal Community at Yarrabah told the Senate:

> Mr President, I ask you and all Australians to recognise that out of 64 senators and all the honourable members who sit in the other place there is only one Aboriginal voice. If that voice is not raised in support of the Indigenous people of this country, there will not be any voice raised.[10]

---

8   Senate, *Hansard*, 19 September 1974, p. 1267.
9   Senate, *Hansard*, 8 December 1976, p. 2791.
10   Senate, *Hansard*, 17 March 1982, p. 914.

Fifty-two years on, there are now 11 Aboriginal voices in our Parliament. Regardless of how many Indigenous voices are in our Parliament, the time has come to ensure that there is a constitutional guarantee of there always being an Indigenous Voice to the Parliament. Let's hope the 11 Indigenous members of the present Parliament can honour the memory of Neville Bonner, convincing their fellow members of all parties to design the constitutional and legislative architecture for an assured Indigenous Voice to the Commonwealth Parliament.

It's now 16 years since John Howard raised the question of constitutional recognition of the First Australians. I am committed to ensuring such recognition in terms acceptable to Indigenous leaders, but I remain of the view that a successful referendum will likely require support from all major political parties in the Parliament. I believe such support will not be forthcoming unless the constitutional constraints on the Voice ensure that it will not clog the courts nor glue up the system of government. This is the challenge in the year ahead, and thus the reason for my writing this book. In so doing I put forward a simplified amendment to what is presently proposed, and I do so in the hope that it might lead to further discussion about the appropriate words for inclusion in the Constitution, words that might result in the Australian people agreeing to a Voice.

CHAPTER ONE
A Task for Every
Conscientious Citizen

I've been a Catholic priest in the public square for many years. People often ask what role there is for a Christian in contemporary political debates, especially with the declining number of Australians who identify as Christian in the census. Being a Catholic, I often receive help from the teaching of the popes – teachings which can make sense and add value for all persons of good will. During the first year of his pontificate, Pope Francis in his Apostolic Exhortation *Evangelii Gaudium* said:

> An authentic faith – which is never comfortable or completely personal – always involves a deep desire to change the world, to transmit values, to leave this earth somehow better that we found it. We love this magnificent planet on which God has put us, and we love the human family which dwells here, with all its tragedies and struggles, its hopes and aspirations, its strengths and weaknesses. The earth is our common home and all of us are brothers and sisters.[1]

Pope Francis then quoted, with approval, his predecessor Pope Benedict who wrote in his encyclical *Deus Caritas Est* that 'the just ordering of society and of the state is a central responsibility of politics', and the Church 'cannot and must not remain on

---

1   Pope Francis, *Evangelii Gaudium*, #183.

the sidelines in the fight for justice'.[2] Pope Francis added this observation:

All Christians, their pastors included, are called to show concern for the building of a better world. This is essential, for the Church's social thought is primarily positive: it offers proposals, it works for change and in this sense it constantly points to the hope born of the loving heart of Jesus Christ.

The recently completed Plenary Council of the Australian Church endorsed the *Uluru Statement from the Heart* and encouraged 'engagement with processes for implementing the statement, including local, regional, and national truth-telling efforts'.[3]

Prior to the 2007 election, John Howard promised that if he won the election he would hold a referendum for the amendment of the Australian Constitution so that it recognised Aboriginal and Torres Strait Islander Peoples in the Constitution. Howard having lost, the new Rudd Labor Government committed itself to consultation on the matter with Indigenous Australians. In 2010, Prime Minister Julia Gillard then set up an Expert Panel which recommended something more substantive than a symbolic preamble. The panel wanted a racial non-discrimination clause placed in the Constitution. Critics saw this as a one line 'bill of rights'. There was no way this proposal could win support in the Parliament. After a round of community consultations, Aboriginal and Torres

---

2   Benedict XVI, *Deus Caritas Est* #28.
3   Fifth Plenary Council of Australia, Draft Decree One, *Reconciliation: Healing Wounds, Receiving Gifts* available at https://plenarycouncil.catholic.org.au/wp-content/uploads/2022/07/FINAL-Decree-1-Reconciliation-Healing-Wounds-Receiving-Gifts.pdf

Strait Islander representatives who gathered at Uluru for the 50th anniversary of the 1967 referendum called for 'the establishment of a First Nations Voice enshrined in the Constitution'.[4]

During successive governments spanning the years 2015–2021, Liberal prime ministers Tony Abbott, Malcolm Turnbull and Scott Morrison ruled out any such proposal. The Albanese government was elected with a commitment to proceed with a referendum. At the Garma Festival in July 2022, Prime Minister Anthony Albanese proposed the following words be placed in the Constitution:

1. There shall be a body, to be called the Aboriginal and Torres Strait Islander Voice.
2. The Aboriginal and Torres Strait Islander Voice may make representations to Parliament and the Executive Government on matters relating to Aboriginal and Torres Strait Islander Peoples.
3. The Parliament shall, subject to this Constitution, have power to make laws with respect to the composition, functions, powers and procedures of the Aboriginal and Torres Strait Islander Voice.[5]

Noel Pearson in the first of his 2022 Boyer Lectures said, 'We know the nation's leader must be joined by all his counterparties in the federal parliament.'[6] For any referendum to succeed, there is a need for a parliamentary process inviting all persons to put forward their proposed wording of any amendment. There will then be a

---

4   *Uluru Statement from the Heart*, Appendix.
5   Anthony Albanese, *Address to Garma Festival*, 30 July 2022 available at https://www.pm.gov.au/media/address-garma-festival
6   Noel Pearson, *Boyer Lecture 1: Recognition*, available at https://about.abc.net.au/speeches/noel-pearson-boyer-lecture-series-who-we-were-and-who-we-can-be/

need for buy-in and ownership of any proposal from both sides of the parliamentary aisle. That is now the task before us. Noel Pearson is confident that 'racism will diminish in this country when we succeed with recognition'.[7] The challenge is to find a formula of words for that constitutional recognition that is acceptable both to Indigenous leaders and to our national leaders on both sides of the parliamentary chamber – thereby increasing the prospects of support of the Australian people.

This cause is just. The going will be tough. We need to concede that there will be people of good will, including some committed Christians, who oppose whatever is ultimately proposed for insertion into our Constitution. But none of us can deny the enormity of the social crisis confronting Indigenous Australians – and all of us as a nation. None of us can deny that previous solutions have not worked. All of us want and need to be attentive to Indigenous Australians who carry the inter-generational trauma of dispossession and colonial disinterest in the cultures which were abused. In the *Uluru Statement from the Heart*, our Indigenous leaders said:

> Proportionally, we are the most incarcerated people on the planet. We are not an innately criminal people. Our children are aliened from their families at unprecedented rates. This cannot be because we have no love for them. And our youth languish in detention in obscene numbers. They should be our hope for the future. These dimensions of our crisis tell plainly the structural nature of our problem. This is the torment of our powerlessness.[8]

---

7   Ibid.
8   *Uluru Statement from the Heart*, Appendix.

I suggest ten steps for Australian Christians inspired by our Catholic social teaching when approaching the forthcoming referendum. For reasons that should be apparent when walking these ten steps, I couch these suggestions in terms appropriate for those of us who are not Indigenous. We are all invited into constructive dialogue. We must strive to listen to community leaders who know what is good for their communities, just as those of us who are not Indigenous know what is good for ourselves and our loved ones.

1. Be attentive to the voices of Aboriginal and Torres Strait Islander people. Stop telling them what is good for them. Start listening to them. Accept that they know what is good for them, just as we know what is good for us and our loved ones.
2. Don't expect all Aboriginal and Torres Strait Islander people to agree about legal, political and constitutional questions. It's called living in a democracy.
3. Form respectful relationships with Aboriginal and Torres Strait Islander people and engage in respectful conversations.
4. Having heard a range of Indigenous voices, make your own decisions about what Aboriginal aspirations are morally justified. What would be right and proper for Australia in the 21st century? For example, the Australian Parliament has power to make special laws about First Nations people. Many Aboriginal people now say, 'No special laws without us!'
5. Know your history; know the history of Aboriginal and Torres Strait Islander peoples. The Australian Constitution does not even mention these peoples. They belong in the Constitution. Their belonging should be explicit and particular.
6. The Constitution belongs to all people. It cannot be amended

except with an overwhelming majority of the people. Educate yourselves about Aboriginal people's aspirations at Uluru and be ready to discuss those aspirations at the family meal, the workplace barbecue, or the local club.

7. Do something to get this issue of constitutional recognition on the right track. Speak to your local member. Ask that parliament set up a process so everyone can have their say so that the major political parties can own whatever is proposed. This is not just a matter for Indigenous leaders. It is not just a matter for the government. It involves all of us.

8. Having decided which Aboriginal people's aspirations are justified, you then need to make a wise decision about which of those aspirations are politically achievable. Don't be afraid to talk to people with varying views when making that decision.

9. Having decided which Aboriginal people's aspirations are not only justified but achievable, you then need to decide to act. You need to put some skin in the game. You need to decide what concrete and just actions you will take. It's not enough just to vote when the referendum comes around. You need to get on board and urge the Parliament to put the right proposition to the vote, and help your fellow citizens make an informed choice.

10. Be respectful and attentive to those who disagree with you, but don't be afraid to demand that they be respectful and attentive to you. Any national Voice worth its salt will have an elaborate system of local and regional ears – to hear the local and regional voices – which are needed to give credibility to any national Voice. That will be complex. There will be plenty of room for disagreement.

Whatever the politics of this referendum, we all need to take to heart Noel Pearson's chilling observation about his people: 'We are a much unloved people. We are perhaps the ethnic group Australians feel least connected to. We are not popular and we are not personally known to many Australians. Few have met us and a small minority count us as friends.'[9] Noel was the original proponent of the Indigenous Voice. Ever since he suggested the idea in September 2014, he has been a key Indigenous leader every step of the way.

I come to this task tentative and respectful, but assured about the key preconditions for achieving constitutional change in Australia. It's for Aboriginal people to tell us what form of constitutional recognition will satisfy them. It's for all of us then to design that form of constitutional recognition to be consistent with the appropriate constitutional architecture, ensuring that the form does not distort the Constitution, does not risk endless litigation in the courts, and does not threaten to clog the workings of government. I take seriously the critique offered of my approach by Noel Pearson in June 2018 when he spoke of me as his 'great and old friend':

> I have known Frank for over 35 years, since I was a very young man, and his commitment to the Aboriginal and Torres Strait Islander people and the cause of reconciliation has been long-held and profound. However, I think the mistake Frank made in this debate and in other debates … [lies in] thinking that reconciliation is about compromise; that Indigenous people should compromise their current position in order to achieve reconciliation. That cannot be

---

9   Noel Pearson, *Boyer Lecture 1: Recognition*, available at https://about.abc.net.au/speeches/
     noel-pearson-boyer-lecture-series-who-we-were-and-who-we-can-be/

the case. For people who have lost everything, how could there be an expectation of further compromise? This is about common ground, locating common ground, and for my taste Frank has mistaken the search for common ground with his predilection for finding compromise. He was mistaken in this and I pray that in the journey that now begins afresh, that he will understand that.[10]

I too pray that I understand. The search for the common ground of constitutional change inevitably involves compromise, not according to one's predilection, but according to the long-acknowledged requirement that constitutional change requires broad cross-party support in our Parliament. Any proposal with minimal risk of ongoing litigation and of clogging the daily processes of government will have an enhanced prospect of winning support from all major political parties. As a nation, we must do better than waiting for another day, hoping for another idea. We have waited and laboured 16 years. It's time to resolve the matter.

Some voters will be committed to voting 'Yes' regardless of the small print in the proposed constitutional amendment. Others will be dyed-in-the-wool 'No' voters regardless of what any lawyer or politician might say about the proposed amendment. But there will be a sizeable group of voters with a natural hesitance about amending our Constitution, preferring, or even demanding, coherent explanations for the 'Yes' case before casting their ballot. It's primarily for them that I write. I hope this book assists those voters in grappling with the issues before making an informed choice at the ballot box.

---

10   Noel Pearson, Launch of Shireen Morris, *Radical Heart*, available at https://www.youtube.com/watch?v=iimDpw-CWT4&t=77s at 2:20-.

CHAPTER TWO
The Australian Constitution and Earlier Amendments

Sometime in 2023 Australian voters will be asked to vote at a referendum amending the Constitution. Americans can tell you some of the things which feature in their Constitution. From the movies, many Australians could also mention some of the features of the US Constitution such as the right to bear arms and the right to plead the Fifth Amendment. Thanks to the movies, most Australians probably know more about the US Constitution than their own. The Australian Constitution, in comparison, is a bland document. It does not include any bill of rights. It sets out the arrangements between the States and the Commonwealth. It also stipulates the roles of parliament, the executive government and the judiciary.

The Australian Constitution is very democratic in at least one dimension. It cannot be amended by the politicians or the judges. It can be amended only by the vote of the people. To amend the Constitution, Parliament has to propose a law passed by both houses (the House of Representatives and the Senate). That proposal is then put to the people at a referendum. The proposal succeeds only if it is supported by an overall majority of the voters and if it is supported by the majority of voters in at least four of the six states.[1]

This double majority requirement helps to explain why it is so difficult to amend the Australian Constitution. There have been 44

---

1   The votes of people living in the ACT, the NT and any of Australia's external territories count towards the national majority only.

attempts since federation in 1901. Only 8 of those attempts have succeeded. Usually, an attempt to amend the Constitution will fail unless it is sponsored or fully supported by the more conservative side of politics. The Labor Party has made 25 attempts to amend the Constitution. It has failed 24 times. Any voter who participated in the successful Labor referendum is now over 97 years old. That referendum held in 1946 allowed the Australian Parliament to make laws with respect to social security payments such as unemployment benefits and family allowances.

The Australian Constitution was drawn up at a series of Constitutional Conventions held at the end of the nineteenth century. Our 'founding fathers' (and they were all men) included some very talented lawyers and statesmen. Their aim was to bring together the six British colonies on the Australian continent, forming a nation which would be a federation of the six states. They not only needed to obtain the agreement of the people in the colonies, but also needed to obtain the approval of the Imperial authorities. The Constitution was then included as part of an Imperial Act of the British Parliament. The preamble of the Imperial Act stated:

> WHEREAS the people of New South Wales, Victoria, South Australia, Queensland, and Tasmania, humbly relying on the blessing of Almighty God, have agreed to unite in one indissoluble Federal Commonwealth under the Crown of the United Kingdom of Great Britain and Ireland, and under the Constitution hereby established:
>
> And whereas it is expedient to provide for the admission into the Commonwealth of other Australasian Colonies and possessions of the Queen.

By the time of federation, Western Australia had also come on board so that there were six colonies to constitute the Commonwealth of Australia.

Under the Constitution, state parliaments retained their power to make laws about all manner of things. But the Australian Parliament was given the power to make laws with respect to particular matters listed in section 51. Those matters included a range of things from defence and external affairs, to banking, railway construction, marriage, and corporations. If there were to be a conflict between a valid law enacted by the Australian Parliament under section 51 and a state law, the Commonwealth law would prevail to the extent of any inconsistency.

The Commonwealth Parliament was given power under section 51(26) to make laws with respect to 'the people of any race, other than the aboriginal race in any state, for whom it is deemed necessary to make special laws'. This provision sounds strange to modern ears. At Federation, those who lived in the Australian colonies were British subjects. This was back in the days of the White Australia policy. Lawmakers wanted to maintain tight supervision of some racial groups who had come to Australia, especially the Chinese who had come to the goldfields and the South Sea Islanders who had been brought as indentured labourers to the sugar cane fields in Queensland. Even if these groups were not to be deported, government wanted to be able to impose restrictions on these racial groups. Given that the Australian Parliament would take control of immigration and emigration, it made sense that the Commonwealth also have the power to impose restrictions on these targeted racial groups. The provision was originally formulated to allow the Australian Parliament to make laws with respect to 'the affairs of people of any race with respect to whom it is deemed necessary to make special laws not applicable to the general community; but so that this power shall not extend to authorise legislation with respect to the aboriginal native race in Australia.'[2]

Henry Bournes Higgins – having migrated with his family from Ireland in 1870 – together with his fellow constitutional founders envisaged that such laws would restrict unwelcome migrants such as Afghans and the Chinese. Australia's first prime minister Edmund Barton told the 1898 Constitutional Convention in Melbourne: 'I entertain a strong opinion that the moment the Commonwealth obtains any legislative power at all it should have the power to regulate the affairs of the people of coloured or inferior races who are in the Commonwealth'.[3]

The founding fathers saw no need for the Commonwealth to take control of First Australians in the states. The politicians from states like Western Australia did not want the Commonwealth to be able to interfere with the policies adopted for dealing with Aboriginal people in remote parts of the country.

One of the other purposes of the Constitution was to provide for the division of revenues amongst the states. Some distribution would be made according to the population of each state. As there were next to no services being provided to First Australians in remote areas, it was decided that there was no need them in the reckoning of population for each state. So, section 127 of

---

2   Clause 53.1, *Commonwealth of Australia Bill*, as adopted by the National Australasian Convention, 9th April, 1891.

3   Edmund Barton, *Official Report of the National Australasian Convention Debates* (Third Session): Melbourne 1898, pp. 228-9.

the Constitution provided: 'In reckoning the numbers of the people of the Commonwealth, or of a state or other part of the Commonwealth, aboriginal natives shall not be counted.'

In the 1960s, there was an increased awareness that the Commonwealth Parliament should take some responsibility for the plight of Aboriginals. It was no longer good enough just to leave the matter to the states. Robert Menzies had been long time prime minister and he was a very competent constitutional lawyer. Even members of his own party were agitating that there should be a referendum to take out the two adverse references to Aboriginals. Everyone agreed that section 127 had reached its use-by date. But section 51(26) was another matter. Menzies pointed out that the Commonwealth power to make laws with respect to the people of a particular race was not a power which usually would be exercised for the benefit or to the advantage of that racial group. The founding fathers intended that the power be exercised, if at all, to restrict the movements and action of groups like the Chinese or the South Sea Islanders. So why would you amend the Constitution to allow the Australian Parliament to make laws adverse to Aboriginals? Why wouldn't you simply leave the matter to the states?

When Harold Holt replaced Menzies as prime minister, advocates renewed their campaign to have section 51(26) amended so that the Australian Parliament would have power to make laws with respect to Aboriginals. They argued that the primary purpose of the change would be to allow the Commonwealth to make laws and implement policies for the benefit of Aboriginals. They won the day and the Holt government agreed to proceed with a referendum. There was unanimous support for the referendum in the Parliament. Usually, the voters in a referendum would be provided with a pamphlet setting out the 'Yes' and 'No' cases for the amendment. Given the unanimity in the Parliament, no one saw the need for a 'No' case. The advertising for the referendum simply stated: 'Vote Yes for Aborigines'. The referendum was carried with overwhelming support in all states. 90.77% of voters voted 'Yes' – the highest vote by far in any referendum since federation.

On one level, the change to the Constitution did not mean very much. It simply omitted the two adverse references to Aboriginals. Aboriginal people were no longer mentioned in the Constitution. The referendum took out the useless section 127. The change to section 51(26) did empower the Australian Parliament to legislate with respect to Aboriginals. But the politicians had assured the voters that the Commonwealth would co-operate with the states on the delivery of services, rather than overriding state policies and approaches. With the election of the Whitlam Labor government five years later in 1972, that changed. Gough Whitlam was committed to the recognition of Aboriginal land rights and to self-determination for Aboriginal communities. The overwhelming vote in the 1967 referendum provided the impetus for change. A symbolic change to the Constitution resulted in real, substantive changes to law and policy.

In 1967 we voted overwhelmingly to extend the operation of an outdated racist provision to include the possibility that the Australian Parliament could legislate with respect to the First Australians. As judges of the High Court have said, the amended provision 'was an affirmation of the will of the Australian people that the odious policies of oppression and neglect of Aboriginal citizens were to be at an end'[4] and 'to mitigate the effects of past barbarism'[5]. The primary object of the power as amended to include Aboriginal peoples was beneficial, removing the fetter upon the legislative competence of the Australian Parliament to pass necessary laws for the benefit of Aboriginal peoples.

Since 1967, governments on both sides of politics have enacted laws in the Australian Parliament in recognition of land rights and indigenous cultural heritage. Laws made pursuant to section 51(26) have usually been intended to be of benefit to Aboriginal and Torres Strait Islander Australians. But there have been some instances when the Australian Parliament has passed a special law and Aboriginals have claimed that the law is detrimental to their interests. Examples of this have included Commonwealth laws dealing with the Hindmarsh Bridge controversy and the Northern Territory intervention implemented by the Howard government.

The absence of any mention of Aboriginals in the Constitution, and the passage of some laws which Aboriginals have found disagreeable, have given rise to calls for explicit recognition of the First Australians in our Constitution. Some Aboriginal leaders and groups have said they would not be content with mere symbolic recognition. They want a place at the table from where they can affect laws and policies relevant to them.

These calls for recognition accompanied the processes for proposing that Australia become a republic in the 1990s. The rationale was that if Australia were to become a republic, there should be suitable recognition and empowerment of Aboriginals as

---

4   Justice Brennan in *The Commonwealth* v *Tasmania (The Tasmanian Dam Case)* (1983) 158 CLR 1 at 242.

5   Justice Deane in *The Commonwealth* v *Tasmania (The Tasmanian Dam Case)* (1983) 158 CLR 1 at 273.

members of that republic. Aboriginal leader Lowitja O'Donoghue was a member of the Republican Advisory Committee set up by Prime Minister Paul Keating and chaired by Malcolm Turnbull. O'Donoghue was the Chair of the Aboriginal and Torres Strait Islander Commission (ATSIC) at the time. She proposed that a new preamble be placed in the Constitution acknowledging Aboriginal history, entitlements and aspirations. This idea was further pursued by O'Donoghue and other delegates at the Republican Convention in 1999.

O'Donoghue convened a working group at the convention favouring the recognition of Indigenous Australians in the preamble. She was joined by Neville Bonner and Gatjil Djerrkura, who had also been the chair of ATSIC. Also on board were self-confessed constitutional conservatives Julian Leeser and Dame Leonie Kramer. Kramer was a senior fellow of the conservative think tank, the Institute of Public Affairs. Leeser later went on to become executive director of the Menzies Research Centre, the Liberal Party's think tank, before becoming a Liberal member of parliament. This meant that a broad cross-section of the delegates had the opportunity to give some thought to the likely shape of any new constitutional preamble. While there was no agreement about Australia becoming a republic, there was unanimity about the need to better recognise Aboriginals in the Constitution, whether or not Australia was ever to become a republic.

When the republican push came to a temporary halt, Indigenous Australians and their supporters continued to point out the lacuna in the Constitution that was silent about them, and that gave no assured place to them at the table of policy development and law making. In time, both sides of politics in the Australian Parliament pledged to do something about it. But ever since, there has been a failure to reach bipartisan agreement on the way forward.

So now to consider the history of those attempts since the dying days of the Howard government in 2007.

CHAPTER THREE
History of Proposals for Indigenous Recognition

2007–2017

In the week before the dissolution of the House of Representatives and the issuing of the writs for the 2007 election, Prime Minister John Howard announced:

> [I]f re-elected, I will put to the Australian people within 18 months a referendum to formally recognise Indigenous Australians in our Constitution – their history as the first inhabitants of our country, their unique heritage of culture and languages, and their special (though not separate) place within a reconciled, indivisible nation. My goal is to see a new Statement of Reconciliation incorporated into the Preamble of the Australian Constitution. If elected, I would commit immediately to working in consultation with Indigenous leaders and others on this task. It would reflect my profound sentiment that Indigenous Australians should enjoy the full bounty that this country has to offer; that their economic, social and cultural well-being should be comparable to that of other Australians. I would aim to introduce a bill that would include the Preamble Statement into Parliament within the first 100 days of a new government. A future referendum question would stand alone. It would not be blurred or cluttered by other constitutional considerations. I would seek to enlist wide community support for a 'Yes' vote.

I would hope and aim to secure the sort of overwhelming vote achieved 40 years ago at the 1967 referendum.[1]

Howard lost the election. His declaration remains the high-water mark of what has been promised by any Liberal prime minister on the issue of Indigenous constitutional recognition. He confined himself only to the prospect of a preamble being inserted into the Constitution, what nowadays is labelled as minimal symbolic change. He never envisaged more substantive change to the Constitution. Kevin Rudd won the 2007 election for the Labor Party. He immediately set about the unfinished business of the parliamentary apology to the Stolen Generations. He promised to address constitutional recognition in his second term. But he was not to enjoy a second term. Julia Gillard toppled him and became prime minister just two months before the 2010 election. Four months after the election, she set up an expert panel on Indigenous recognition. The panel – chaired by the Father of Reconciliation, Patrick Dodson, and lawyer Mark Leibler – reported in January 2012. This expert panel included well known key Indigenous leaders including Mick Gooda, Marcia Langton, Ken Wyatt, Noel Pearson, Megan Davis, and Les Malezer.

The panel adopted four principles 'to guide its assessment of proposals for constitutional recognition of Aboriginal and Torres Strait Islander peoples, namely that each proposal must:

---

1   John Howard, Address to the Sydney Institute, 11 October 2007 at https://parlinfo.aph.gov.au/parlInfo/search/display/display. w3p;query=Id%3A%22media%2Fpressrel%2FL41P6%22;src1=sm1

1. contribute to a more unified and reconciled nation
2. be of benefit to and accord with the wishes of Aboriginal and Torres Strait Islander peoples
3. be capable of being supported by an overwhelming majority of Australians from across the political and social spectrums
4. be technically and legally sound.'[2]

This was undoubtedly the correct approach and these four principles hold true today. Unfortunately, the panel proposed a series of measures which I argue (below) did not comply with the third principle and possibly the fourth principle. The panel recommended that a new section 116A be inserted in the Constitution:

(1) The Commonwealth, a State or a Territory shall not discriminate on the grounds of race, colour or ethnic or national origin.

(2) Subsection (1) does not preclude the making of laws or measures for the purpose of overcoming disadvantage, ameliorating the effects of past discrimination, or protecting the cultures, languages or heritage of any group.[3]

There was strong opposition, particularly within the Coalition parties in parliament, to any proposal which would arm judges with the constitutional power to determine whether any law or policy was racially discriminatory or whether any law or policy was permissibly discriminatory because it was made 'for the purpose of overcoming

---

2 *Recognising Aboriginal and Torres Strait Islander Peoples in the Constitution: Report of the Expert Panel,* January 2012, p. 4.
3 Ibid, p. 231.

disadvantage, ameliorating the effects of past discrimination, or protecting the cultures, languages or heritage of any group'. For the Coalition, these were policy decisions to be made by an elected parliament and not by an unelected judiciary.

It was surprising that the Expert Panel recommended this section 116A. Key members of the panel had been involved in the parliamentary debates following the High Court *Mabo* and *Wik* decisions. In 1993, the Keating government was steering its *Native Title Act* through the Senate. In 1998, the Howard government was negotiating with Senator Brian Harradine in the Senate to enact comprehensive reforms and additions to the *Native Title Act*. Each time, a key sticking point was the relationship between the *Native Title Act* and the *Racial Discrimination Act*. Each time, government insisted that there was a need for the *Native Title Act* being a later, more specific Act to prevail over the general provisions of the *Racial Discrimination Act* so as to render certain the grant of other titles especially to miners and pastoralists. Each time, the Greens and Democrats in the Senate tried to ensure that the *Racial Discrimination Act* would prevail over the *Native Title Act* whenever there was a conflict between the two. Each time, the government insisted that such an amendment would blow apart the certainty of the whole native title regime. In 1998, even the Labor Party in opposition could not bring itself to support the Democrats' amendment because of its 'so-called clause busting capacity'[4].

The Expert Panel's proposed section 116A would have been the equivalent of placing the Greens' 1993 and 1998 amendments into the Constitution. There would have been no way to ensure certainty of all other land titles until the High Court had the opportunity

---

4   Senate, *Hansard*, 6 July 1998, p. 5037.

to interpret the application of section 116A. When the Whitlam Government had the *Racial Discrimination Act* passed through the Australian Parliament in 1975, everyone knew that it would bind the states, but that the Australian Parliament would still have the capacity to legislate specifically to override the application of the *Racial Discrimination Act*. Both the Keating and Howard governments exploited that capacity in relation to native title so as to produce an outcome workable and acceptable for all parties including miners and pastoralists.

With the proposed section 116A being the central plank of the Expert Panel's recommendations, there was no way that their report was ever going to develop any political traction. They flouted their third principle, and arguably their fourth principle. Their recommendations were not 'capable of being supported by an overwhelming majority of Australians from across the political and social spectrums'[30].

When considering process and timing for a referendum, the Expert Panel was right to recommend:

> Before making a decision to proceed to a referendum, the Government should consult with the Opposition, the Greens and the independent members of Parliament, and with State and Territory governments and oppositions, in relation to the timing of the referendum and the content of the proposals.
>
> The referendum should only proceed when it is likely to be supported by all major political parties, and a majority of State governments.[5]

---

5   *Recognising Aboriginal and Torres Strait Islander Peoples in the Constitution*: Report of the

With the central plank of the Expert Panel's recommendations section 116A having been cast aside, the Gillard government together with the Abbott Opposition attempted to salvage some of the good work that had been done. The Parliament unanimously passed the *Aboriginal and Torres Strait Islander Peoples Recognition Act 2013* stating:

1. The Parliament, on behalf of the people of Australia, recognises that the continent and the islands now known as Australia were first occupied by Aboriginal and Torres Strait Islander peoples.
2. The Parliament, on behalf of the people of Australia, acknowledges the continuing relationship of Aboriginal and Torres Strait Islander peoples with their traditional lands and waters.
3. The Parliament, on behalf of the people of Australia, acknowledges and respects the continuing cultures, languages and heritage of Aboriginal and Torres Strait Islander peoples.[6]

Prime Minister Gillard told Parliament:

Expert Panel, p. 227 (terms of reference issued in December 2010 and report delivered in January 2012).

6   S. 3, *Aboriginal and Torres Strait Islander Peoples Recognition Act 2013*. This echoed the recommendations of the Expert Panel which thought there should be a new provision in the Constitution:
    Recognising that the continent and its islands now known as Australia were first occupied by Aboriginal and Torres Strait Islander peoples;
    Acknowledging the continuing relationship of Aboriginal and Torres Strait Islander peoples with their traditional lands and waters;
    Respecting the continuing cultures, languages and heritage of Aboriginal and Torres Strait Islander peoples.

At the election of 2007, it seemed that the prospect of constitutional recognition was very close at hand, supported as it was by both major parties. But, in difficult and volatile times, we have not found the settled space in our national conversation to make the promised referendum a reality. So, the government has advanced this bill for an act of recognition, to assure Indigenous people that our purpose of amendment remains unbroken and to prepare the wider community for the responsibility that lies ahead.[7]

In response, Tony Abbott said:

There is much hard work to be done. It will, as the Prime Minister candidly admitted, be a challenge to find a form of recognition which satisfies reasonable people as being fair to all. It will not necessarily be straightforward to acknowledge the First Australians without creating new categories of discrimination, which we must avoid because no Australians should feel like strangers in their own country. I believe that we are equal to this task of completing our Constitution rather than changing it.[8]

Then Shadow Attorney General George Brandis had the carriage of the Bill for the Opposition in the Senate. He said that the foreshadowed referendum could be the necessary bookend to the 1967 referendum, warning:

---

7   House of Representatives, *Hansard*, 13 February 2013, p. 1121.
8   Ibid, p. 1123.

But it will only succeed – and this is acknowledged by all participants – if it has widespread community support; not just bipartisanship – for referendums have sometimes failed despite having bipartisan support – and not just support from the Aboriginal and Torres Strait Islander communities but support across the whole of the Australian community. Which means that it is just as important that people with conservative views be persuaded as people who consider themselves to be progressives. If that is to happen the proposal must be modest and the tone of the debate must be respectful.

Nothing is surer to defeat the referendum than if the public discussion of the proposal is conducted in a hectoring, angry or righteous manner.[9]

Brandis was Deputy Chair of the 2013 Joint Select Committee on Constitutional Recognition of Aboriginal and Torres Strait Islander Peoples. This was chaired by Labor's Northern Territory Senator Trish Crossin, who spoke of the need for 'a strong multi-partisan parliamentary consensus on the specific content, wording and timing of a referendum proposal'[10].

When Tony Abbott defeated Kevin Rudd at the polls in 2013, the report of the Expert Panel was consigned to the dustbin because the racial non-discrimination clause could be categorised simplistically as a one-clause bill of rights. Abbott was publicly committed to some form of constitutional recognition but not any

---

9   Senate, *Hansard*, 26 February 2013, pp. 868-9.
10   Joint Select Committee on Constitutional Recognition of Aboriginal and Torres Strait Islander Peoples, *Progress Report*, June 2013, para. 3.19.

provision that would arm the judges with overarching oversight of parliament's Indigenous affairs policies. On New Year's Day 2014, he said, 'I will start the conversation about a constitutional referendum to recognise the first Australians. This would complete our Constitution rather than change it.'[11]

Noel Pearson turned his mind to what meaningful constitutional recognition might look like in the absence of a non-discrimination clause as proposed by the Expert Panel (of which he was a key member) and rejected by the Liberal and National Parties both when in opposition and in government. In September 2014, Pearson published a *Quarterly Essay* entitled 'A Rightful Place: Race, Recognition and a More Complete Commonwealth' in which for the first time he floated the idea of 'the Voice':

> [C]onservatives should agree with the removal of racial discrimination from the Constitution. They believe in national unity and dislike internal divisions, separatism and collectivism. They must now also turn their minds to how the Constitution might be altered so that the discrimination of the past cannot happen again. We don't want separatism: we want inclusion on a fair basis. We want to be inside the decision-making tent. We want our voices to be heard in political decisions made about us. A mechanism like this – guaranteeing the Indigenous voice in Indigenous affairs – could be a more democratic solution to the racial discrimination problem.

---

11   Tony Abbott, *Media Release 23189*, 1 January 2014, available at https://pmtranscripts. pmc.gov.au/release/transcript-23189

Constitutional recognition could therefore include removal of the race clauses and the insertion of a replacement power to enable the Commonwealth parliament to pass necessary laws with respect to Indigenous peoples, and incorporation of a requirement that Indigenous peoples get a fair say in laws and policies made about us. A new body could be established to effect this purpose and to ensure that Indigenous peoples have a voice in their own affairs.[12]

With his *Quarterly Essay* under his arm, Pearson did the rounds of Liberal cabinet ministers proposing the idea of a Voice. He met with Malcolm Turnbull on 2 June 2015. According to Shireen Morris who was working for Pearson, Turnbull, '… expressed sympathy with the "one-clause bill of rights" arguments against what the Expert Panel proposed, and told us the Indigenous constitutional body alternative "seems sensible". He then asked, "How can I help?"'[13]

Prime Minister Tony Abbott and Opposition Leader Bill Shorten met with 40 Aboriginal and Torres Strait Islander leaders from around the country on 6 July 2015 at Kirribilli House. It was clear to everyone in the room that the proposals submitted by the Expert Panel in January 2012 would not fly. In the lead-up to the Kirribilli House meeting, Marcia Langton and Noel Pearson had blown my proposals in *No Small Change* out of the water, making it clear that modest symbolic change was not an option. They were not interested in deleting the outdated section

---

12   Noel Pearson, *A Rightful Place: Race, Recognition and a More Complete Commonwealth* (Quarterly Essay, Issue 55, September 2014) pp. 66-7.
13   Morris, Shireen. *Radical Heart*, Melbourne University Press, 2018, p. 145.

25 which was a provision limiting state representation in the House of Representatives if a state were to discriminate against voters on the basis of race. They were not interested in a new preamble or acknowledgment at the commencement of the Constitution. They were not concerned about any rewording section 51(26). For them, all options other than the Voice were off the table. Instead, from their perspective the primary need was to reboot the process for constitutional recognition.

The Indigenous participants noted the four principles set down by the Expert Panel in 2012 but they went on to insist that they were seeking substantive and not symbolic change to the Constitution. Taking their lead from Pearson's and Langton's earlier statements, they said, 'A minimalist approach, that provides preambular recognition, removes section 25 and moderates the races power [section 51(26)], does not go far enough and would not be acceptable to Aboriginal and Torres Strait Islander peoples.' They said that 'any reform must involve substantive changes to the Australian Constitution. It must lay the foundation for the fair treatment of Aboriginal and Torres Strait Islander peoples into the future.'[14] They floated Pearson's idea of 'a new advisory body established under the Constitution'.

Tony Abbott put in motion the machinery to establish the Referendum Council. Then, returning from his annual visit to remote Aboriginal communities in Cape York, Abbott gave an interview to the respected, now deceased journalist, Michael Gordon who reported: 'Tony Abbott has warned advocates of

---

14 'Statement presented by Aboriginal and Torres Strait Islander attendees at a meeting held today with the Prime Minister and Opposition Leader on Constitutional Recognition', HC Coombs Centre, Kirribilli, Sydney, Monday, 6 July 2015. See http://www.austlii.edu.au/au/journals/ILB/2015/37.pdf

strong constitutional recognition for Indigenous Australians they will "probably end up with a proposal that won't pass" if they go for everything they would like in the referendum question. The Prime Minister has also made plain that he does not support Noel Pearson's proposal for an Indigenous advisory body to be enshrined in the Constitution, saying the Parliament could establish such a body if it was deemed necessary.'[15]

The ABC's Elizabeth Jackson then asked Noel Pearson about Michael Gordon's report in *The Age* that morning: 'He says that he won't support your idea of an Indigenous advisory body to be enshrined in the Constitution. What's your reaction to that decision?' Pearson replied:

Yeah, I found that very strange, Elizabeth, because only last week we agreed on a process of Indigenous conferences and consultations with Australians, a proper process over 12 months where nothing was to be ruled in and out. And then I find this puzzling commentary from the Prime Minister, ruling some models out even before we've started the consultation.

Jackson put to him: 'So you're suggesting that he's told you one thing and told the journalist something else?' Noel Pearson replied: 'Well, that's the way I read it. And I think Michael Gordon's piece in *The Age* makes very clear where he stands on the issue.'[16]

---

15 Michael Gordon, 'Indigenous recognition: Tony Abbott says pushing for big changes to constitution will fail', *The Sydney Morning Herald*, 29 August 2015, available at https://www.smh.com.au/politics/federal/indigenous-recognition-tony-abbott-says-pushing-for-big-changes-to-constitution-will-fail-20150828-gj9xpc.html

16 ABC, *AM*, 29 August 2015. See http://www.abc.net.au/am/content/2015/s4302446.htm

Abbott could not have been clearer. Gordon could not have been clearer. A Voice enshrined in the Constitution was just not a goer for any government led by Tony Abbott, regardless of what any Referendum Council might propose, regardless of what Indigenous leaders might rule in or out. An impasse was reached. By mutual agreement, everyone had ruled out section 116A. The Aboriginal leaders had ruled out all other options other than the Voice in the Constitution. The Prime Minister had ruled out the Voice in the Constitution. There was no common ground left.

Two months later, Malcolm Turnbull replaced Abbott as Leader of the Liberal Party and Prime Minister. In December 2015, both sides in Parliament endorsed the appointment of a 16-member Referendum Council chaired once again by Mark Leibler and Patrick Dodson who had chaired the 2012 Expert Panel. Turnbull led the government to a double dissolution election in July 2016. Patrick Dodson had to step aside as co-chair when he became a Labor Senator for Western Australia. He was replaced by Pat Anderson. Other Indigenous leaders on the council included once again Noel Pearson and Megan Davis. During the election campaign, Turnbull and leader of the Opposition Bill Shorten said they would await the recommendations of the Referendum Council. No one tried to resuscitate the recommendations of the 2012 Expert Panel.

In his autobiography *A Bigger Picture*, Malcolm Turnbull vividly recalls the meeting he then hosted with Aboriginal leaders including the four Aboriginal members of Parliament (Labor members Patrick Dodson, Linda Burney and Malarndirri McCarthy and Liberal member Ken Wyatt) and Labor leader Bill Shorten on 25 November 2016 after a meeting of the Referendum Council.

Noel Pearson 'said that he was expecting the Uluru conference to recommend that there be a change to the Constitution to establish "a Voice", which would be a national advisory assembly composed of and elected by Aboriginal and Torres Strait Islander peoples'.[17]

According to Turnbull:

A general discussion followed and there wasn't a lot of support for the Voice around the room. Shorten and I both expressed the same view: we weren't comfortable with the Constitution establishing a national assembly open only to the members of one race, and moreover we both said we thought it would have no prospect of success in a referendum. 'A snowball's hope in hell,' as Bill had previously said to me.[18]

Shorten has never denied having said this. Turnbull reports that things turned rather sour after the meeting:

I returned across the corridor to my office and Pearson followed me. He then became very angry, stood very close and started to swear at me because I hadn't agreed with him. I didn't respond in kind. 'Noel, you can recommend whatever you wish – you're entitled to my honest opinion, not my acquiescence.' Pearson abused Ken Wyatt and Pat Dodson when they spoke to him later that afternoon. He seemed furiously indignant that everyone hadn't agreed with him.

---

17 Malcolm Turnbull, *A Bigger Picture*, Hardie Grant, 2020, p. 570.
18 Ibid, p. 571.

Turnbull's account of the incident is consistent with, though milder than, the ABC's published report of the proceedings.[19] It's important to note that this showdown between Pearson and Turnbull took place before any of the 13 Dialogues hosted by the Referendum Council to ascertain the views of local Aboriginal and Torres Strait Islander communities in the lead up to the Uluru meeting in May 2017. Pearson was adamant that the Voice was the only option. All other options were off the table. Just like Abbott, Turnbull and Shorten were adamant that a constitutionally entrenched Voice was not a goer.

---

19 The ABC report of the incident was not published until 5 June 2017, after the Uluru meeting. See https://www.abc.net.au/news/2017-06-05/pearsons-alleged-tirade-at-pm-over-constitutional-recognition/8583158

CHAPTER FOUR
The *Uluru Statement* and the Referendum Council

2017

Between 1993 (when Lowitja O'Donoghue put ATSIC's preamble to the Republican Advisory Committee) and 2007 (when John Howard promised a new preamble should he be re-elected), the talk of constitutional recognition was largely confined to discussion about the contents of any new preamble to the Constitution, or to the Imperial Act to which the Constitution was attached. The Expert Panel which reported in 2012 wanted to supplement symbolic recognition with a substantive constitutional provision outlawing racial discrimination. By 2015, everyone accepted that a non-discrimination clause was not a goer, and key Indigenous leaders – notably Marcia Langton and Noel Pearson – had ruled out minimalist solutions such as the repeal of section 25, the reworking of section 51(26), and any preamble or acknowledgment of Indigenous history, present reality and aspirations.

Just prior to the 25th anniversary of *Mabo* and the 50th anniversary of the 1967 constitutional referendum, 250 First Nations people gathered in May 2017 at Uluru in the centre of Australia. The purpose of their gathering was to consider how they might best be recognised in the Australian Constitution which does not even mention them nor the history of their ancestors. They issued the *Uluru Statement from the Heart* telling us that Aboriginal sovereignty is 'a spiritual notion'. They told us:

[The] ancestral tie between the land, or 'mother nature', and the Aboriginal and Torres Strait Islander peoples who were born therefrom, remain attached thereto, and must one day return thither to be united with our ancestors. This link is the basis of the ownership of the soil, or better, of sovereignty.

Not many 21st century Aboriginal Australians use terms like therefrom, thereto and thither. This statement is an adapted quote from the submission put by Mr Bayona-Ba-Meya, Senior President of the Supreme Court of Zaire, who appeared on behalf of the Republic of Zaire in the International Court of Justice in 1975 dismissing 'the materialistic concept of *terra nullius*' substituting 'a spiritual notion'. Judge Fouad Ammoun, the Lebanese Vice-President of the International Court, quoted the submission in his judgment in the *Advisory Opinion on Western Sahara*.[1] This part of Judge Ammoun's

---

1   Following is the relevant part of Judge Ammoun's decision [1975] ICJR at pp. 77-8:
    'Anyone familiar with the philosophy of Zeno of Sidon or Citium and his Stoic school cannot but be struck by the similarity between the ideas of that philosopher and the views of Mr. Bayona-Ba-Meya as to the links between human beings and nature, between man and the cosmos. Further, the spirituality of the thinking of the representative of Zaire echoes the spirituality of the African Bantu revealed to us by Father Placide Tempels, a Belgian Franciscan, in his work *Philosophie bantoue*. The author sees therein a "striking analogy" with "that intense spiritual doctrine which quickens and nourishes souls within the Catholic Church".
    'Mr. Bayona-Ba-Meya goes on to dismiss the materialistic concept of *terra nullius*, which led to this dismemberment of Africa following the Berlin Conference of 1885. Mr. Bayona-Ba-Meya substitutes for this a spiritual notion: the ancestral tie between the land, or "mother nature", and the man who was born therefrom, remains attached thereto, and must one day return thither to be united with his ancestors. This link is the basis of the ownership of the soil, or better, of sovereignty. This amounts to a denial of the very concept of *terra nullius* in the sense of a land which is capable of being appropriated by someone who is not born therefrom. It is a condemnation of the modern concept, as defined by Pasquale Fiore, which regards as *terrae nullius* territories inhabited by populations whose civilization, in the sense of the public law of Europe, is backward, and whose political organization is not conceived according to Western norms.'

46

opinion was then quoted by a couple of the judges in the High Court *Mabo* decision.

How extraordinary that the inheritors of the longest living culture on earth would quote a Lebanese judge quoting a lawyer from Zaire to express the depths of their spiritual relationship with the land. This is a profound lesson for those of us seeking an inclusive Australia. We are able to share our diverse cultural and religious modes of expression to communicate the deepest yearnings of our hearts. Judge Ammoun observed in his judgment that the 'spirituality of the thinking of the representative of Zaire echoes the spirituality of the African Bantu revealed to us by Father Placide Tempels, a Belgian Franciscan, in his work *Philosophie bantoue*. The author sees therein a "striking analogy" with "that intense spiritual doctrine which quickens and nourishes souls within the Catholic Church".' How extraordinary it is too, that remarks by Muslim lawyers from Zaire and Lebanon echoing African Bantu and Belgian Catholic notions of spirituality would come to express Australian Indigenous spiritual aspirations to land in such a foundational document.

All 13 Dialogues prior to the Uluru meeting endorsed the Pearson proposal for a Voice. At Uluru, the delegates all agreed to a resolution calling for 'the establishment of a First Nations Voice enshrined in the Constitution'[2]. They put aside all previous suggestions such as any proposed preamble, the repeal of section 25, or a reworking of section 51(26), the race power. These options were seen as minimal symbolic proposals which were not worthy of consideration.

The Coalition government rejected the idea of a constitutionally entrenched Voice out of hand. Just three days after Uluru, the

---

2   *Uluru Statement from the Heart*, Appendix.

Deputy Prime Minister Barnaby Joyce labelled such a Voice as a third chamber of the parliament.[3] Three months later, the Turnbull Cabinet which included the Coalition's leadership team of Scott Morrison, Barnaby Joyce, Josh Frydenberg and Peter Dutton unanimously resolved that:

The Government does not believe such an addition to our national representative institutions is either desirable or capable of winning acceptance in a referendum. Our democracy is built on the foundation of all Australian citizens having equal civic rights – all being able to vote for, stand for and serve in either of the two chambers of our national Parliament ... the House of Representatives and the Senate. A constitutionally enshrined additional representative assembly for which only Indigenous Australians could vote for or serve in is inconsistent with this fundamental principle ... [T]he Government does not believe such a radical change to our constitution's representative institutions has any realistic prospect of being supported by a majority of Australians in a majority of States.[4]

Australians desiring constitutional recognition would do well to consider Amanda Vanstone's qualifying statement to the report of the Referendum Council of which she was a member. Amanda

3   *The Guardian*, 29 May 2017 at https://www.theguardian.com/australia-news/2017/may/29/barnaby-joyce-criticised-for-misinterpreting-proposed-indigenous-voice-to-parliament

4   Joint Media Release of Malcolm Turnbull, George Brandis and Nigel Scullion, 26 October 2017, available at https://parlinfo.aph.gov.au/parlInfo/download/media/pressrel/5596294/upload_binary/5596294.pdf;fileType=application%2Fpdf#search=%22media/pressrel/5596294%22

Vanstone, having been a Minister for Indigenous Affairs and a moderate Liberal in Cabinet, observed:

If Parliament and the Australian people want to progress with constitutional recognition of first Australians the consultations have made clear that a voice to Parliament is not so much the best shot at it but that it is the only shot in the locker. This is a relatively new development. If that were not the case Indigenous leaders speaking on behalf of Indigenous Australians would have said so some time ago. That means despite all the effort, contributions and time expended over a number of years we now find ourselves at a new starting point. Exhausting as that may seem to some that's where we are.[5]

In her typically no-nonsense way, Vanstone went on to say:

It would be a folly to take the support previously expressed by Australians for Constitutional Recognition in the Constitution to be unconditional. Whilst one would expect that Australians would not support something which Indigenous Australia did not endorse it is not clear that they would automatically endorse whatever Indigenous Australia prefers. The substantive change contemplated is quite different from what had been contemplated by everyone and everyone will have to refresh their thinking.[6]

---

5   *Final Report of the Referendum Council*, 30 June 2017, p. 65.
6   Ibid.

Vanstone bluntly and honestly expressed her view that the model 'which has been discussed, is not one I believe would be acceptable to the majority of Australians.'[7] She pointed the way to the future:

The task therefore is to find a version of an Indigenous voice to parliament that will be acceptable to Indigenous Australians and the parliament of the day. That debate, the one that gets to the basics of what would be acceptable to both Indigenous Australia and the Parliament should be had before a referendum is contemplated.[8]

The theoretical problem we all now confront was nicely posited by Aboriginal legal academic Megan Davis writing 13 years ago when the preamble was the main symbolic constitutional change on offer. She would embrace minimal symbolic change only if it led to substantive constitutional change. She and her co-author Zrinka Lemezina wrote:

It seems that the preamble will either be a discrete forerunner to substantive constitutional provisions or a mechanism that allows us to sidestep these uncomfortable elements of Australian life. To achieve proper recognition of Indigenous people, we need to resist the allure of the preamble as a panacea to the shortfalls of Australian public law: for it to mean anything at all, we must demand something more substantial than a socio-political teaching

---

7   Ibid, p. 66.
8   Ibid, p. 67.

aid, or a mechanism for legal edification. It is important that, in discussing constitutional recognition of Aboriginal and Torres Strait Islander peoples, we do not allow the feel good factor of public education to supersede structural change. While greater civic awareness is a laudable achievement in its own right, ultimately public advocacy for a more inclusive preamble must assist in the long-term goal of constitutional reform. To the extent that the preamble debate supplements this greater conversation, it is a welcome development. But we must guard against reform that, in effect, obfuscates and distracts from substantive issues of 'Unfinished Business'.[9]

On 12 February 2018 the Leader of the Opposition, Bill Shorten, in his Closing the Gap remarks told Parliament:[10]

In this parliament, we owe it to move past misleading scare campaigns and get recognition back on track ... Members of this parliament mightn't feel totally comfortable with, or were surprised by, what was proposed at Uluru, but in this place we don't get to choose what the people tell us. In this place, we listen to what the people tell us and we implement their will. And let me also be very straight – we want bipartisanship. But bipartisanship cannot mean an agreement to do nothing. It cannot be used as an alibi for the lowest common denominator. I ask the government to reconsider their rejection of the Statement from the Heart.

---

9   Megan Davis & Zrinka Lemezina, 'Indigenous Australians and the Preamble: Towards a More Inclusive Constitution or Entrenching Marginalisation?', 33 *University of New South Wales Law Journal* 239, (2010), p. 265.

10   House of Representatives, *Hansard,* 12 February 2018, p. 928.

But, if we cannot work on this together, the next Labor government will, instead, as a first step, look to legislate the Voice to Parliament.

Shorten went on to say:

We will begin the detailed design work in opposition, work with Uluru delegates and many other first-nations people who've led the thinking on this issue. And, if we form a government, we will sensibly move to finalise legislation which establishes the voice and includes a clear pathway to constitutional change, enshrining that basic principle that you don't make decisions about people without talking to them. In fact, I think it will be easier for a referendum to succeed and harder for a scare campaign to be run, if we already have lived legislative experience of such a body.

Shorten's proposal and rationale continue to attract support. Alas, that route was not taken. It was opposed outright by the Indigenous leaders. No doubt, they were aware of the problems there had been over the decades with the establishment and then the abolition of the National Aboriginal Consultative Committee (NACC) (1972-1977), the National Aboriginal Conference (NAC) (1977-1985), ATSIC (1990-2004) and most recently the National Congress of Australia's First Peoples (2010-2019).

During 2018, a parliamentary committee was set up to pursue the recommendations of the Referendum Council. The committee was co-chaired by Julian Leeser from the Liberal Party and the highly respected Indigenous leader, Patrick Dodson, from the Labor

Party. The terms of reference for the joint committee required that they:

> … recommend options for constitutional change and any potential complementary legislative measures which meet the expectations of Aboriginal and Torres Strait Islander peoples and which will secure cross party parliamentary support and the support of the Australian people.[11]

Three of the key leaders from Uluru – Pat Anderson, Megan Davis and Noel Pearson – proposed to the parliamentary committee that there be a First Nations Voice to present its views to government as well as to the Parliament. This was a significant change. They suggested that the Voice be able to present views not just on proposed laws made under sections 51(26) and 122 but on all 'matters relating to Aboriginal and Torres Strait Islander peoples'.[12] Their suggested amendment to the Constitution was proposed well after the cut-off date for receipt of submissions. This meant that there was little opportunity for other citizens to scrutinise their suggestion and put forward changes.

As joint chairs of the parliamentary committee, Dodson and Leeser wrote:

> Beyond the poetry of the *Statement from the Heart* is the prose of political reality – the need to ensure that our

---

11 Joint Select Committee on Constitutional Recognition relating to Aboriginal and Torres Strait Islander Peoples, *Final report*, November 2018, Resolution of Appointment, p. xiii.

12 Pat Anderson, Noel Pearson, Megan Davis et al., Joint Select Committee on Constitutional Recognition relating to Aboriginal and Torres Strait Islander Peoples, Submission 479, 3 November 2018, p. 6.

recommendations provide for a form of constitutional recognition that is legitimate and acceptable to Aboriginal and Torres Strait Islander peoples as well as our parliamentary colleagues across the spectrum, and ultimately to the Australian people.[13]

They went on to say:

Leaving aside any questions of the need to build further political consensus, it is difficult to proceed to referendum today on The Voice when this Committee has received no fewer than 18 different versions of constitutional amendments which might be put at a referendum.[14]

Patrick Dodson is now the Albanese Government's Special Envoy for Reconciliation and the Implementation of the *Uluru Statement from the Heart*. Julian Leeser is the Shadow Minister. The committee also included as members Linda Burney and Malarndirri McCarthy who are now, respectively, the Minister and Assistant Minister for Indigenous Australians.

Back in 2018, Dodson, Burney and McCarthy put their name to a report emphasising 'the importance of cross-party support to achieve constitutional change'.[15] They noted:

The fact that there are so many different provisions proposing to constitutionalise The Voice and that a new

---

13   Joint Select Committee on Constitutional Recognition relating to Aboriginal and Torres Strait Islander Peoples, *Final report*, November 2018, p. vii.
14   Ibid, pp. viii-ix.
15   Ibid, p. 2, para 1.10.

provision was suggested in a late submission received by the Committee on 3 November 2018, nearly two months after submissions had closed, indicates that neither the principle nor the specific wording of provisions to be included in the Constitution are settled. More work needs to be undertaken to build consensus on the principles, purpose, and the text of any constitutional amendments.[16]

That's been the last bipartisan utterance we've heard from our elected leaders.

Eight months after the parliamentary committee reported, Murray Gleeson – who had been Chief Justice of Australia and a member of the Referendum Council – said:

It is difficult to see any objection in principle to the creation of a body to advise Parliament about proposed laws relating to Indigenous affairs, and specifically about special laws enacted under the race power which, in its practical operation, is now a power to make laws about Indigenous people.[17]

But note he was speaking about a body with a far more confined purpose than that proposed by the key advocates from Uluru.

The retired chief justice and member of the Referendum Council also sounded a salutary warning note: 'I think it very likely that Australians, and Parliament itself, would want to see what the

---

16 Ibid, p. 118, para 3.143.
17 Murray Gleeson, *Recognition in Keeping with the Constitution: A Worthwhile Project*, Uphold and Recognise, 2019, p. 12.

body looks like, and hear what the Voice sounds like, before they vote on it'[18]. This was precisely what Bill Shorten had been saying as Leader of the Opposition.

For nearly five years, both sides of politics seem to have given up on bipartisan co-operation and due parliamentary process. There has been no further parliamentary co-operation 'to build consensus on the principles, purpose and the text of any constitutional amendments'. After the 2019 election, Barnaby Joyce apologised for describing the Voice as a third chamber, but he reiterated, 'What I do say – we've got to take this debate forward ... take the debate forward in a form that succeeds. There's no point going to a referendum with something that is not going to work.'[19]

On 17 March 2021, Noel Pearson delivered a significant address at the National Museum, appealing to the better instincts of the Liberal Party and invoking their senior statesman, John Howard. He put to his national audience the question: What is it that we are engaged in, and have been [engaged in] ever since Prime Minister John Howard made the commitment at the beginning of the 2007 Federal Election campaign?'[20]

Pearson conceded that Howard had never signed up to an Indigenous Voice recognised in the Constitution. Howard was merely proposing what the advocates would now describe as symbolic, namely any recognition of Indigenous peoples through the insertion of a preamble in the Constitution acknowledging 'their history as the first inhabitants of our country, their unique

---

18   Ibid.
19   *The Guardian*, 18 July 2019 at https://www.theguardian.com/australia-news/2019/jul/18/barnaby-joyce-apologises-for-calling-indigenous-voice-a-third-chamber-of-parliament
20   Noel Pearson, *It's time for constitutional recognition*, 17 March 2021, at https://capeyorkpartnership.org.au/its-time-for-true-constitutional-recognition/

heritage of culture and languages, and their special (though not separate) place within a reconciled, indivisible nation'[21].

Whatever hopes there were that this National Museum Address might open the Liberal National Party Government to a new round of meetings were short-lived. For his part, Scott Morrison was quite unyielding. At a press conference the day after Noel Pearson's address, Morrison was asked: 'Are you willing to consider going to a referendum to enshrine a Voice into the Constitution or do you rule that out?' Morrison answered: 'We already have. It has never been the Government's policy to have that process enshrined in the Constitution. That never has been the Government's policy. I think that is pretty clear. It is not the Government's policy.'[22]

Until this time, Noel Pearson had put considerable faith in John Howard. On 21 April 2021, Pearson told the ABC audience that Abbott, Turnbull and Morrison had dropped the ball. Harking back to earlier times, Pearson said, 'It's 13 years since John Howard launched constitutional recognition as an agenda. He said on the eve of the election that his party if re-elected would act within 18 months of the election. So had Howard won in 2007, this would all be history.'[23] But like his three successors, Howard never endorsed the idea of the Voice to Parliament being inserted into the Constitution. If he were to do so, that would be a real game changer. Were Howard and Pearson to agree, the terms of any such agreement would be sure to honour the four principles

---

21 John Howard, Address to the Sydney Institute, 11 October 2007 at https://parlinfo.aph.gov.au/parlInfo/search/display/display. w3p;query=Id%3A%22media%2Fpressrel%2FL41P6%22;src1=sm1

22 Transcript, *Press conference*, 18 March 2021, see https://pmtranscripts.pmc.gov.au/release/ transcript-43278

23 Noel Pearson, *ABC TV Breakfast*, 21 April 2021 available at https://www.youtube.com/ watch?v=8tXUYfARAIA at 4:25

first enunciated by the Expert Panel. Tony Abbott indicated that he was open to some recognition of Indigenous people in the Constitution, while continuing to ask: '[B]ut does this really entail the constitutional entrenchment of a new entity giving some, but not others, their own unique "voice" to parliament?'[24]

On 11 July 2021, Professor Marcia Langton, the co-chair of the Senior Advisory Group to Government on the co-design of the Indigenous Voice, delivered the *B'nai B'rith Human Rights Oration* reflecting on the *Uluru Statement from the Heart*. The 19-member Senior Advisory Group had worked with a National Co-design Group and a Local and Regional Co-design Group. All up, the groups included 52 members. Langton put forward a view that in the political climate of the time, the most nuanced approach would be to legislate prior to an ultimate referendum. She told the audience which included Mark Leibler:

'The almost unanimous view of our 52 members is that our proposal should be legislated as soon as possible and we should not wait for a federal government to finally reach the conclusion that a referendum should be held. Let me be clear: the present government under the Prime Minister Scott Morrison is opposed to holding a referendum. It is not clear either if Morrison's government supports the Voice proposal we have designed.

Given this predicament, again let me be clear with you: I am not here to advocate for a referendum on constitutional enshrinement of a Voice for Indigenous Australians to have

---

24 Tony Abbott, 'Teaching for best selves not governments', in Greg Craven, *Shadow of the Cross*, Kapunda Press, 2021, p. 64.

a say in matters that affect them in laws and policies – at least not at this stage of history. Although I support the *Uluru Statement from the Heart*, the present government, as I said, is opposed to it. By proposing to delay our design for an Indigenous Voice to Parliament and to government until some unknown date in the future, those advocates for the *Uluru Statement from the Heart* are delaying the only chance we have at present for a mechanism for a Voice – a legislated mechanism. And I remind you, most Aboriginal and Torres Strait Islander people want a Voice established as a matter of priority. They did not tell us that they want it delayed until there is a referendum. I'm here to advocate to you that you consider the report of the Indigenous Voice Codesign Group and support legislation for the Voice mechanism that we have designed over the last 18 months.

I hope that in the next few years we will be able to jointly support a referendum but in the face of a government that opposes a referendum and will not indicate if it supports an Indigenous Voice, we have only one option: a legislated mechanism for a Voice as soon as possible.[25]

Despite assurances from then Minister for Indigenous Australians Ken Wyatt, the Morrison Government took no steps towards legislating the Voice in any form. Revisiting the history of his fraught relationship with Turnbull, Noel Pearson said in April 2022:

---

25   Marcia Langton, *B'nai B'rith Human Right Oration*, 11 July 2021, available at https:// www.youtube.com/watch?v=fgwOKr64YP4

So the position he adopted in 2017 wasn't the position he had two years prior when I went to see him. So the complete turnaround of course he'd adopted Barnaby's formula about the Voice being a third chamber and he wouldn't back down on that. It wasn't his characterisation of this idea. It was Barnaby Joyce's. So yeah my respect for Malcolm completely plummeted after 2017 when he took the position he did. It was an outrageous lie, outrageous misrepresentation of the Voice idea but thankfully the idea has survived him.[26]

It must be conceded that Turnbull's opposition to a constitutionally entrenched Voice long predated Barnaby Joyce's post-Uluru declaration that it would be a third chamber. Turnbull's position was firmly entrenched, and even shared by Bill Shorten as Opposition leader, and that was prior to the community dialogues and the *Uluru Statement from the Heart*.

Before the election of the Albanese government, Marcia Langton was sensibly proposing a legislated Voice as a precursor to constitutional recognition. Bill Shorten as leader of the opposition had supported such a pragmatic approach. No Liberal Prime Minister was prepared to take the next step towards legislation, let alone constitutional recognition.

---

26   Noel Pearson in conversation with Paul Keating, Judith Neilson Institute for Journalism and Ideas, 6 April 2022, https://podcasts.apple.com/au/podcast/listen-at-jni/id1615713303?i=1000556479238

CHAPTER FIVE
Mr Albanese at Garma

2022

After the 2019 election, Bill Shorten resigned as leader of the Labor Party. Anthony Albanese took over the leadership in May 2019. The ALP 2021 National Platform published in preparation for the 2022 election stated that 'we cannot look to the future without coming to terms with our past. That must start by listening to the generosity of the *Uluru Statement from the Heart* and acting – including through a Voice to Parliament enshrined in the Constitution.'[1]

Albanese's Budget Reply Speech on 31 March 2022 was seen as the first salvo in the 2022 election campaign. Anthony Albanese did not confine himself to economic issues. He pledged to move promptly on the *Uluru Statement from the Heart*. He told Parliament:

> I want an Australia of boundless opportunity, an inclusive Australia that celebrates our rich diversity and values our multiculturalism as an asset, an Australia that embraces the generous *Uluru Statement from the Heart*, including [through] a constitutionally recognised Indigenous Voice to this parliament.[2]

---

1   ALP National Platform 2021 at https://alp.org.au/media/2594/2021-alp-national-platform-final-endorsed-platform.pdf, p. 2.
2   House of Representatives, *Hansard*, 31 March 2022, p. 149.

This was a clear point of differentiation with the Coalition whose last three leaders had firmly rejected the prospect of a Voice to Parliament being included in the Constitution.

On election night, Prime Minister Albanese's opening words in his victory speech on 21 May 2022 were:

I begin by acknowledging the traditional owners of the land on which we meet. I pay my respects to their elders past, present and emerging. And on behalf of the Australian Labor Party, I commit to the *Uluru Statement from the Heart* in full.

Later in his speech, he said:

Together we can be a self-reliant, resilient nation, confident in our values and in our place in the world. And together we can embrace the *Uluru Statement from the Heart*. We can answer its patient, gracious call for a Voice enshrined in our constitution. Because all of us ought to be proud that amongst our great multicultural society we count [as] the oldest living continuous culture in the world.

For many years it has been traditional for new prime ministers and leaders of the opposition to attend the Garma Festival as guests of Aboriginal leader and traditional owner Galarrwuy Yunupingu – a prominent leader and strong voice for Aboriginal people. This festival – on Yolgnu lands in Arnhem Land in the Northern Territory – is one of Australia's largest Indigenous gatherings. Albanese attended the 2022 Festival and made a major announcement there on 30 July 2022: 'Today, I re-affirm my government's solemn promise to implement the *Uluru Statement from the Heart*, in full.'[3] He described the Voice in these terms:

> Enshrining a Voice in the Constitution gives the principles of respect and consultation, strength and status. Writing the Voice into the Constitution means a willingness to listen won't depend on who is in government or who is Prime Minister. The Voice will exist and endure outside of the ups and downs of election cycles and the weakness of short-term politics. It will be an unflinching source of advice and accountability. Not a third chamber, not a rolling veto, not a blank cheque. But a body with the perspective and the power and the platform to tell the government and the parliament the truth about what is working and what is not. To tell the truth – with clarity, with conviction. Because a Voice enshrined in the Constitution cannot be silenced.

He went on to say:

> Our starting point is a recommendation to add three sentences to the Constitution, in recognition of Aboriginal and Torres Strait Islanders as the First Peoples of Australia:
> - There shall be a body, to be called the Aboriginal and Torres Strait Islander Voice.
> - The Aboriginal and Torres Strait Islander Voice may make representations to Parliament and the Executive

---

3   Anthony Albanese, Speech at Garma, 30 July 2022, https://www.pm.gov.au/media/address-garma-festival

Government on matters relating to Aboriginal and Torres Strait Islander Peoples.

- The Parliament shall, subject to this Constitution, have power to make laws with respect to the composition, functions, powers and procedures of the Aboriginal and Torres Strait Islander Voice.

He was careful not to close the door on further discussion and refinement of the words. But he was keen to indicate that there was only one door open, and the room for movement was slight. He said:

These draft provisions can be seen as the next step in the discussion about constitutional change. This may not be the final form of words – but I think it's how we can get to a final form of words. In the same way, alongside these provisions, I would like us to present the Australian people with the clearest possible referendum question. We should consider asking our fellow Australians something as simple, but something as clear, as this: 'Do you support an alteration to the Constitution that establishes an Aboriginal and Torres Strait Islander Voice?'

He welcomed the attendance of Julian Leeser, the Shadow Minister. But there was no indication of an openness to a bipartisan approach. Presumably the previous rejection of the Voice by all three Liberal Prime Ministers gave Albanese little hope of getting the Opposition on board. Peter Dutton, the Leader of the Opposition, had been conspicuous by his absence from Parliament when Kevin

Rudd proposed the apology to the Stolen Generations in 2008. The one glimmer of light was that Dutton now admitted that his 2008 absence was a mistake and he studiously avoided making any comment on the Voice, other than to request further details from government. Such a request from an opposition leader is quite proper and reasonable.

Other members of the Coalition were not for 'keeping their powder dry'. Even before Albanese spoke at Garma, the newly elected Aboriginal Coalition Senator from the Northern Territory, Jacinta Price, was on the front foot. In her maiden speech to the Senate, she said: 'This government has yet to demonstrate how this proposed Voice will deliver practical outcomes and unite rather than drive a wedge further between Indigenous and non-Indigenous Australia.'[4]

Within a week of Albanese's appearance at Garma, Tony Abbott launched into print saying: 'Everything about the proposed Voice drips with entrenching separatism as an atonement for dispossession even though Indigenous people can never expect to achieve Australian outcomes without also embracing Australian standards.'[5]

The challenge is to convince conservatives that a constitutional advisory body is desirable, and perhaps even necessary, and that it will not drive a wedge further between Indigenous and non-Indigenous Australia and will not entrench separatism.

---

4   Senate *Hansard*, 27 July 2022, p. 120, also available at https://www.jacintaprice.com/maiden-speech

5   Tony Abbott, 'Entrenching race in Constitution drives us further apart', *The Australian*, 3 August 2022 available at https://www.theaustralian.com.au/commentary/entrenching-race-in-constitution-drives-us-further-apart/news-story/7795a21d3ff052b2fd4a89f90a62e36f

Conservative critics of the Voice seem to be suggesting that there is never a need to make special laws for Aboriginals and Torres Strait Islanders and thus there is never a need to make special provision for the way they are to be consulted. Nothing could be further from the truth. Constitutional conservatives should agree that section 51(26) of the Constitution which allows the parliament to make laws 'with respect to the people of any race for whom it is deemed necessary to make special laws' is a fairly outdated provision. Aboriginals and Torres Strait Islanders are the only Australians subject to such special laws in the twenty-first century.

Usually these laws relate specifically to Aboriginal issues such as land rights, native title, cultural heritage, and Indigenous languages. If parliament is to make such special laws, surely those Australians who are the custodians of this heritage and the holders of these distinctive rights should be consulted.

Sometimes these 'special laws' are enacted on other issues which are not uniquely Indigenous, such as laws restricting access to alcohol. But then these laws are made applicable only to Aboriginal and Torres Strait Islander peoples, being classed as special measures under the *Racial Discrimination Act*. For example, the recently lapsed *Northern Territory National Emergency Response Act 2007* which, among other things, established grog bans on remote communities in the Northern Territory provided that: 'The provisions of this Act, and any acts done under or for the purposes of those provisions, are, for the purposes of the *Racial Discrimination Act 1975* , special measures.' Such special measures are not extended to any other racial groups in contemporary Australia. If such measures are to be enacted in the twenty-first century, there ought to be some constitutional mechanism for ensuring consultation with the affected racial group.

The primary constitutional function of the Voice should be to provide a means by which Aboriginal and Torres Strait Islander peoples are consulted prior to the enactment of laws which apply specially to them. This may either may be either because the laws relate to distinctive Indigenous issues such as land rights, native title, cultural heritage, and Indigenous languages, or because the laws are special measures targeted at Aboriginal and Torres Strait Islander peoples. These laws may appear racially discriminatory, but they are designed to enhance the situation of a disadvantaged racial group (under the *Racial Discrimination Act* consistent with the UN *Convention on the Elimination of All Forms of Racial Discrimination*).[6] Unlike the situation at the turn of the twentieth century, no other group in the community today is subject to the Commonwealth's distinctive law-making power under section 51(26) and no other group in the community is subject to the special measures regime under the UN Convention. This 'special' regime of law making applies only to Aboriginals and Torres Strait Islanders. Even constitutional conservatives – perhaps especially constitutional conservatives – should be attentive to the Indigenous cry of: 'No more special laws about us unless we are consulted.'

As the Indigenous leadership has abandoned any call for amending the 'race' provisions in the Constitution (sections 25 and 51(26)), the only issue on the table for consideration is the addition

---

6   Article 1(4) of the *International Convention on the Elimination of All Forms of Racial Discrimination* provides: 'Special measures taken for the sole purpose of securing adequate advancement of certain racial or ethnic groups or individuals requiring such protection as may be necessary in order to ensure such groups or individuals equal enjoyment or exercise of human rights and fundamental freedoms shall not be deemed racial discrimination, provided, however, that such measures do not, as a consequence, lead to the maintenance of separate rights for different racial groups and that they shall not be continued after the objectives for which they were taken have been achieved.'

of a new constitutional provision for a Voice. However, it should be noted that the 2018 parliamentary joint committee did record its belief that 'there would be broad political support for recognition of Aboriginal and Torres Strait Islander peoples comprising:

- the repeal of section 25; and
- the rewording of section 51(26) to remove the reference to "race" and insert a reference to "Aboriginal and Torres Strait Islander peoples".'[7]

In the wake of Mr Albanese's appearance at Garma, some advocates for the Voice continued to insist that there was no longer a need to work for bipartisan support in the Parliament. They thought the referendum could be won with a strong government message being backed by a far-reaching social media campaign and a media campaign funded by corporate Australia. They drew parallels with the 2018 Australian Marriage Law Postal Survey which attracted 62 per cent support from those who voted. But there are some key differences.

First, voting was not compulsory in the Marriage Law Postal Survey where the turnout was less than 80 per cent of voters. Voting is compulsory in the referendum. Second, the message in the same-sex marriage debate was simple. The proponents asked the public to vote for an outcome which would ensure that marriage be available to all Australians and not just those who are heterosexual. In the 2023 referendum, the voters are being asked to support a measure which provides a special place or support for Indigenous Australians

---

7   Joint Select Committee on Constitutional Recognition relating to Aboriginal and Torres Strait Islander Peoples, *Final Report*, November 2018, para 4.59.

– a Voice to Parliament and perhaps also to Government, a Voice which has no equivalent for other Australians. Third, there were no high-profile LGBT advocates campaigning against a 'Yes' vote in the postal survey. There are some very eloquent, experienced Indigenous leaders campaigning against a 'Yes' vote in the referendum, and for the good of their own people as they see it. Fourth, most people know a gay person, whether a relative or friend, but many Australians do not have such a relationship with even one Indigenous person. Fifth, there are many voters prepared to support a change of law or policy on a contested topic while being naturally wary about amending the Constitution, subscribing to the mantras, 'If you don't know, vote "No"', and 'If it ain't broke, don't fix it.'

CHAPTER SIX
Seeking a Way Forward

At the end of 2022, much of the public debate about Indigenous recognition in our Constitution went pear-shaped, and with a mark of nastiness which was not only unbecoming but also unhelpful. Marcia Langton and Noel Pearson launched quite vindictive attacks on Jacinta Price. Pearson said that Price was trapped in a 'redneck celebrity vortex' and was being used by right-wing think tanks to 'punch down on other black fellas'.[1] When the National Party announced its opposition to the Voice, Langton said:

> It would be terribly unfortunate for all Australians if the debate sinks into a nasty eugenicist, 19th-century style of debate about the superior race versus the inferior race, and I have to say I'm terribly disappointed that a Warlpiri or a Celtic-Warlpiri person has kicked this off.[2]

Jacinta Price in turn attacked Minister Linda Burney for visiting remote communities in private planes wearing Gucci.

1   *The Guardian*, 29 November 2022, available at https://www.theguardian.com/australia-news/2022/nov/29/david-littleproud-is-a-kindergarten-kid-whose-nationals-will-be-left-behind-on-voice-noel-pearson-says
2   *The Australian*, 5 December 2022, available at https://www.theaustralian.com.au/nation/divisive-race-politics-must-end-marcia-langton/news-story/494dad47cc447b8c9834a8dd2ddae010

If ever there was a public policy issue requiring respectful engagement, this is it. We all need to redouble our efforts to have our politicians return to a bipartisan approach, following the appropriate steps for a successful referendum. Now that the Albanese government has put a proposal on the table, there is a need for return to bipartisanship, parliamentary procedure and civil public discourse so that we might accord just constitutional recognition to Indigenous Australians.

Some in the government and in the Aboriginal leadership seem to take the view that the intransigent opposition of three previous Liberal prime ministers negates the possibility of any bipartisan co-operation. They may be right, but I beg to differ. There are members of the Liberal and National parties who share the concern of trying to find a solution to Indigenous constitutional recognition – a concern that spans the last 16 years. There is no point in trying to design a formula for recognition other than one acceptable to Indigenous Australians. But the design must ensure that the representations made by any Voice are not regularly the subject of legal proceedings and are not likely to clog unduly the workings of government. It's in the interests of every political party to have the matter resolved and in a way that does not do violence to the architecture of the Constitution.

Some of our leaders seem to have forgotten that most of their predecessors committed themselves to bipartisan co-operation on this issue for 9 years between 2010 and 2018. Back in 2010, Julia Gillard led a re-elected Labor team to the election, but she needed to cut deals with the Greens and a couple of independents. Each of those deals included a commitment to a referendum on constitutional recognition of Aboriginal and Torres Strait Islander Australians.

Prime Minister Gillard set up the *Expert Panel on Recognising Aboriginal and Torres Strait Islander Peoples in the Constitution* which included 'members of Parliament from across the political spectrum'[3], for a process that required 'collaboration with Parliamentarians from across the political spectrum'.[4]

In 2013, Julia Gillard worked closely with Tony Abbott as Leader of the Opposition for the unanimous passage through Parliament of the *Aboriginal and Torres Strait Islander Recognition Act*.

Labor won the May 2022 election with a strong commitment to the *Uluru Statement*, knowing that all three previous Liberal Prime Ministers had rejected the idea of a Voice being placed in the Constitution. At the Garma Festival in July, the Prime Minister unilaterally announced his intention to adopt the provision put forward in the late submission to the 2018 committee, proposing those words for insertion in the Constitution with a little non-transparent tweaking. For his part, Opposition Leader Peter Dutton has sat back simply asking for more detail. Neither Albanese nor Dutton appear to have reached across the despatch box for the good of the country which has now spent 16 years committed to constitutional recognition but with no agreement on the principles, purpose and text of any constitutional amendment.

We all need to urge politicians on both sides of the parliamentary aisle to return to a bipartisan approach and a transparent parliamentary process for determining the proposed wording to be placed in the Constitution. The first step will be for

---

3   *Expert Panel on Recognising Aboriginal and Torres Strait Islander Peoples in the Constitution*, January 2012, p. 2.
4   Ibid, p. 3.

the government to subject Mr Albanese's Garma set of words to a rigorous parliamentary committee process so everyone can have their say.

If the proposal to be put to the people is to differ substantially from that recommended by the Referendum Council in 2017, it should be the result of a bipartisan parliamentary process. It's time for Messrs Albanese and Dutton to show goodwill reaching across the parliamentary chamber on this issue as did their predecessors Gillard and Abbott, Abbott and Shorten, and Turnbull and Shorten. This might help avoid the repetition of the very unseemly, unhelpful remarks we've heard from experienced people who know that hateful *ad hominem* remarks are not the building blocks of constitutional change. To amend the Australian Constitution, everyone needs to be assured that their voices have been respectfully heard.

Indigenous leaders like Megan Davis and Noel Pearson remain adamant that they are seeking substantive constitutional change, and not just minimal or symbolic changes. Yet if their arguments had been invoked during the 1967 referendum campaign, I fear the 1967 changes would have been rejected by the Indigenous leadership as mere symbolism or minimalist changes and would not have received overwhelming public support. The only changes made in 1967 were to omit the two adverse references to 'Aborigines'.

The political lesson of 1967 is that minimal symbolic change, carried overwhelmingly by the Australian people can be the catalyst for substantive policy and legal changes as occurred when the Commonwealth took over the conduct of Aboriginal affairs. But symbolic constitutional change being a catalyst for substantive policy change is no longer an option. The Indigenous leaders have taken that option off the table.

In November 2022, Noel Pearson devoted almost half of his second Boyer Lecture entitled *A Rightful but Not Separate Place* to John Howard. Pearson rightly sees Howard as pivotal to the response to be made by more conservative Australians coming to vote in this year's referendum. He is trying to lock Howard into a Voice to Parliament and executive government on all matters relating to Aboriginals and Torres Strait Islanders, arguing that the proposal is the result of a fully participative democratic process. Howard is having none of it, and arguably for good reason. As Amanda Vanstone, a member of the Referendum Council, has rightly said, it was Aboriginal leaders who took every constitutional option other than the Voice off the table. It was disavowed by three Liberal prime ministers in a row. The Referendum Council recommended:

That a referendum be held to provide in the Australian Constitution for a representative body that gives Aboriginal and Torres Strait Islander First Nations a Voice to the Commonwealth Parliament. One of the specific functions of such a body, to be set out in legislation outside the Constitution, should include the function of monitoring the use of the heads of power in section 51 (26) and section 122. The body will recognise the status of Aboriginal and Torres Strait Islander peoples as the first peoples of Australia.[5]

They said the Voice to the Parliament should primarily be about the special laws which Parliament makes for Aboriginal and Torres Strait Islander peoples on issues such as native title, heritage protection, and things of that sort. But the Referendum Council

---

5   *Final Report of the Referendum Council*, 30 June 2017, p.2.

did see that the Voice might have more work than that to do. The Referendum Council appreciated the problem of specifying the scope of the Voice's ambit in the Constitution but did not provide an answer. They observed:

[I]t would not be realistic to provide advice on all matters 'affecting' Aboriginal and Torres Strait Islander peoples because most laws of general application affect such peoples. On the other hand, it may be too narrow to limit the subject matters to laws with respect to Aboriginal and Torres Strait Islander peoples because some laws of general application have particular impact on or significance to such peoples.[6]

In the 21st century, Aboriginals and Torres Strait Islander peoples are perfectly entitled to be concerned about anything and everything which parliament or the government is dealing with. So that has become the problem. It was a small group of Aboriginal leaders and legal academics who expanded the Referendum Council's recommendation from a Voice to Parliament on special laws applicable to Aboriginals and Torres Strait Islanders, to a Voice to Parliament and executive government able to make representations on all matters relevant to Aboriginal and Torres Strait Islander peoples. It's this recharacterisation of the Voice which Pearson claims to be the result of democratic process, leaving the rest of us, including John Howard, with no decent option other than unqualified endorsement.

In his second Boyer Lecture, Pearson said:

---

6   Ibid., p. 36.

Howard's 2007 proposal for constitutional reform was subjected to the democratic processes of the national government and parliament ... Aboriginal and Torres Strait Islander communities and their leaders submitted to these processes and sought to advocate and influence the evolving proposals for recognition. This process included engagement with the succession of Liberal and Labor prime ministers who followed.

In his speech to The Sydney Institute on election eve 2007, John Howard was candid about the breakdown in dialogue between himself as Prime Minister and Indigenous leaders. He accepted his share of the blame for it. It was clearly something he felt keenly had been a problem with his government. It is this dialogue that the Voice is directed at: the establishment of a formal body to speak with the prime minister and the executive government of the day and to the parliament.

It could not be the case that the personal preference of an individual – whether a past leader or citizen – could so peremptorily discard the outcome of fifteen years of democratic process. That some leaders have changed their minds from support to opposition, while others have changed from opposition to support, is not really the point. The point is the Voice proposal was the outcome of the Referendum Council, the bi-partisan establishment of which took place during Tony Abbott's government and finalised by Malcolm Turnbull.

Aboriginal people are entitled to expect that Australia's Westminster system obliges members of parliament to respect the outcome of serious democratic deliberation

77

undertaken with hope and sincerity by the least powerful community in that system.[7]

I think it's called poking the bear! John Howard emerged from his cave of isolation and gave an interview to Paul Kelly at *The Weekend Australian*. Kelly is a well-informed journalist who has covered this issue closely from day one. The fact that Howard decided to give an interview to Paul Kelly is indicative because until then Howard had held his fire. Howard said:

I think there are substantial arguments against the Voice. Among people I see as part of the Liberal base I don't find any reaction to the Voice other than one of hostility. Not everyone talks about it. But those who talk about it are critical. My sense is that people are suspicious of the idea of a Voice. I don't get the impression the Voice is something that is going to unite the country the way the 1967 referendum did, because that was just so palpably fair, whereas people are suspicious of the Voice. People saw the 1967 referendum as a demonstration of our good faith. But people see the Voice as creating potential divisions.[8]

Kelly noted: 'On Indigenous recognition, Howard said his position was essentially the same as in 2007. He was still in favour of altering the Constitution in relation to the preamble but acknowledged that Indigenous leaders such as Pearson saw this as inadequate.'

7   Noel Pearson, *Boyer Lecture 2*, https://capeyorkpartnership.org.au/noel-pearson-boyer-lecture-two/
8   *The Weekend Australian*, 19 November 2022 at https://www.theaustralian.com.au/inquirer/john-howards-sway-the-former-pm-speaks-out-on-the-voice/news-story/158cfa50dc66392b61c73d0e4225e122

Pearson was invited to respond when interviewed by Patricia Karvelas on ABC *RN Breakfast* on 29 November 2022:

[T]he position with Howard now is that he may not agree with where the constitutional policy discussion has ended. It ended with a voice. He may not have, he may say, 'No I had a different idea back in 2007.' But who can arrogate to themselves that kind of presumption that their own views should be the view that prevails. We've gone through 15 years of process, 15 years of political history, since Howard kicked off the ball on constitutional recognition, and we've landed with a voice. And we landed with a voice under a Liberal National Party government. You know we landed on the voice before Labor was elected this year. So it's just a matter of people like Howard respecting more than a dozen years of process, inquiry, research, parliamentary committees, reports being delivered to the parliament and so on. We've gone too long on this history of this over a dozen years, and we've landed with the simple idea of a voice, the simple proposition that Aboriginal people should be able to tell the parliament their views on any laws that affect them. That is the simple and modest proposition we landed on. That under the aegis of a Liberal National Coalition government. And we should go forward on that basis.[9]

Pearson was instrumental not only in proposing the Voice all those years ago. He was instrumental in having all other options

---

9   ABC *RN Breakfast*, 29 November 2022 at 12:41-14:50: https://www.abc.net.au/
     radionational/programs/breakfast/noel-pearson-blasts-nationals-the-voice/101709376

taken off the table way back in 2015. The Uluru Dialogues confirmed this one and only option. It was never an option embraced by Howard, Abbott, Turnbull or Morrison. When it was rejected by the Turnbull cabinet, all key senior ministers put their name to the statement of reasons for rejecting it.

There is still a lot of work to do if there is to be any prospect of a successful referendum which can be said to be one that is true towards Indigenous people who have put to us the mode by which they want to be recognised in the Constitution. They have said they want a Voice. Despite Noel Pearson's bold claims, our parliament is yet to debate and decide whether it be a Voice to Parliament or a Voice to Parliament AND government, or a Voice just about particular laws or a Voice about all manner of things. Mr Howard seems to be saying that a Voice of any sort in the Constitution is not on. I dare say he hasn't lost all his political clout. So, we've got a lot of work to do with our fellow citizens if we are serious about responding to the call which has been made in good faith to us by the Indigenous leadership now over a considerable period of time.

For previous referendums our parliamentarians usually provided a pamphlet to the voters setting out the 'Yes' and 'No' case. Each case would be authorised by parliamentarians aligned with that side of the argument. In 1967, there was unanimity in our parliament, and it was decided to provide only a 'Yes' case. This helps to explain the 91 per cent 'Yes' vote in 1967.

This time around, the Albanese government has decided not to provide such a pamphlet. The government has announced:

The next referendum will be the first in the digital age. There is no longer any need for taxpayers to pay for a pamphlet to be sent to every household. Modern technology allows parliamentarians to express their views to voters directly and regularly through a wide variety of sources, such as television, email and social media, that did not exist when the pamphlet was introduced in the early 20th century.[10]

This is a curious decision, given that this referendum relates most especially to Aboriginal and Torres Strait Islander peoples – many of whom living in remote communities are deprived of ready access to email and social media.

The government has also announced: 'To support community education, the Government proposes to temporarily lift a funding restriction in the Act, to enable funding of educational initiatives to counter misinformation. The Government believes campaigns in the Voice Referendum should be organised and funded by the Australian community.'

In the October 2022 Budget, the government intervened in the usual processes and announced that 'Australians for Indigenous Constitutional Recognition', a body campaigning for a 'Yes' vote at the forthcoming referendum, would be granted Deductible Gift Recipient status. Groups such as the Institute of Public Affairs have complained that the government has not provided a similar benefit to any group wanting to campaign for a 'No' vote.[11] There is no

---

10   Mark Dreyfus, Linda Burney and Patrick Dodson, 'Next steps towards Voice Referendum', *Joint Media Release*, 1 December 2022, https://ministers.ag.gov.au/media-centre/next-steps-towards-voice-referendum-01-12-2022

11   Daniel Wild, 'We're Not Fighting a Fair Fight on The Voice to Parliament after Uneven Budget Funding for the "Yes" Vote', Institute of Public Affairs, 29 October 2022, available at https://ipa.org.au/ipa-today/were-not-fighting-a-fair-fight-on-the-voice-to-parliament-after-uneven-budget-funding-for-the-yes-vote

way this referendum will be carried unless the Australian public is convinced that both sides of the argument are being given a fair go.

CHAPTER SEVEN
The 'Yes' Case

Given that the government has decided not to provide voters with a pamphlet setting out the 'Yes' and 'No' case, I believe it's useful now to attempt to do that. Given that the issue is an Indigenous Voice, it is imperative that the reader hear directly from Indigenous voices. In these next two chapters, Indigenous voices will be complemented by those of two retired High Court judges who have expressed contrary views about the legal certainty and justiciability of Mr Albanese's Garma formula. I will add Tony Abbott's voice to the 'No' case as he raises important questions about governance for the good of all Australians.

With the background provided in this book, I trust that these two chapters will be an aid for the informed voter wanting to make a conscientious decision to vote yes or no. I am at pains to present fairly the thinking of key advocates, most especially the Indigenous advocates.

Three of the key Indigenous leaders at Uluru were Megan Davis, Pat Anderson and Noel Pearson.

Megan Davis is a law professor and an appointed expert with the UN Human Rights Council's Expert Mechanism on the Rights of Indigenous Peoples based in Geneva. She brings many years of international experience to her advocacy for the Voice. She was a member of the 2012 Expert Panel and a member of the 2017 Referendum Council. She writes:

The Voice to Parliament is a common feature in many liberal democracies around the world. It is a simple proposition: that Indigenous peoples should have a say in the laws and policies that affect their lives and communities. The idea is that if you have direct Indigenous input into law and policy making, the quality of advice will be vastly better than contemporary decision making which is primarily done by non-Indigenous people making decisions about communities they have never visited and people they do not know. This is why so many communities are not flourishing. This is why so many Aboriginal and Torres Strait Islander people are struggling. The decisions made about their lives are crafted by people in Canberra or other big cities …

The task ahead now is to agree to the amount of detail that is required for Australians to feel fully informed when voting at the ballot box. The full-blown Voice design can be legislated after a successful referendum — such a deferral of detail is a common constitutional and political strategy around the world …

The Voice to Parliament reform is intended to bring security and certainty to people's lives, that we believe will manifest in better outcomes for communities. Being constitutionally enshrined, the Voice will be sustainable and durable well beyond political timetables. It means that Indigenous empowerment and active participation in the democratic life of the nation is not dependent on which political party is in power.

The second reason for constitutional entrenchment is that it is intended to compel government to listen. Currently the government and policy makers are not compelled to hear what First Nations have to say about the laws and policies that affect them. Entrenchment will mean listening to mob is compulsory and allowing Indigenous input into policy will be mandated. This will mean that laws and policies are more likely to be targeted and tailored to community problems and needs — and it will mean laws and policies are less likely to fail.[1]

Noel Pearson, the principal architect of the Voice, was a member of the Gillard Government's 2012 Expert Panel, a member of the Turnbull Government's 2017 Referendum Council and a member of the Morrison Government's 2020 Senior Advisory Group. He delivered the 2022 Boyer Lectures, the first of which was largely dedicated to the Voice. In that lecture entitled *Who We Were, Who We Are, And Who We Can Be,* he outlined Anthony Albanese's Garma announcement and conceded: 'We know the nation's leader must be joined by all his counterparties in the federal parliament, and in the parliaments of the states, and communities across the country – but our hearts are hopeful.'[2] He went on to describe:

> ... a bridge to join all Australians in common cause, to work together in partnership to make a new settlement that celebrates the rightful place of Indigenous heritage

---

1   Megan Davis, 'A First Nations Voice to Parliament: Our plea to be heard', *ABC Opinion,* 27 May 2022, available at https://www.abc.net.au/religion/megan-davis-voice-to-parliament-our-plea-to-be-heard/11300474

2   Noel Pearson, *Boyer Lecture 1*: 'Who We Were, Who We Are, and Who We Can Be', 31 October 2022, available at https://capeyorkpartnership.org.au/noel-pearson-boyer-lecture-one/

in Australia's national identity. A constitutional bridge to create an ongoing dialogue between the First Peoples and Australian governments and parliaments, to close the gap between Indigenous and non-Indigenous Australians.

He made these observations culminating in a thought experiment which he put to listeners if they were to witness Aboriginal elders convening on the bank of the Hawkesbury River where the Queensland boat the *Lucinda* was docked, with the key founding fathers on board drafting the Australian Constitution:

Constitutional recognition will endure but the legislative details can be changed by the parliament if and when it chooses to do so.

Of all the claims I will make in these lectures this is the boldest and one of which I am most convicted: racism will diminish in this country when we succeed with recognition. It will not have the same purchase on us: neither on the majority party that has defaulted to it over two centuries, nor the minority that lives it, fears it and who too often succumb to the very fear itself.

The Australian Constitution moved from negative exclusion to neutral silence. But the 1967 referendum was not positive recognition.

Australia doesn't make sense without recognition. Until the First Peoples are afforded our rightful place, we are a nation missing its most vital heart.

A 'Yes' vote in the Voice referendum will guarantee that Indigenous peoples will always have a say in laws and policies made about us. It will afford our people our rightful place in the constitutional compact. This constitutional partnership will empower us to work together towards better policies and practical outcomes for Indigenous communities.

Constitutional recognition of Indigenous Australians is not a project of identity politics, it is Australia's longest standing and unresolved project for justice, unity and inclusion.

If these representations included the constitutional recognition of Aboriginal and Torres Strait Islander peoples through a Voice to the Parliament and Executive Government in order to create a dialogue between the old and new Australians in respect of the country's heritage and its future – what would those on board the Lucinda respond with the benefit of our hindsight today? I ask each of us: what would our response be if we were on board the Lucinda?

Pat Anderson, the long-time Chair of the Lowitja Institute where she has led research and advocacy on Aboriginal health issues, was Co-Chair of the 2017 Referendum Council and the respected elder who led the Uluru Dialogues. She writes:

Since the advent of colonisation, the absence of an effective process for conducting dialogues between the broader community and First Nations people has been a festering sore at the heart of Australian society.

The *Uluru Statement from the Heart* advocates for a process of dialogue to set us on a path towards a new way

87

of living together. The statement was agreed to in 2017 by a convention of more than 250 First Nations people after an inclusive and rigorous process of regional dialogues. It proposes a First Nations Voice to Parliament to guide a passage both to a new 'coming together' and to the clear articulation of the long-suppressed truth.

Establishing the Voice will lead to immediate, important outcomes. It will set the scene for addressing the centuries of injustice. It will create an effective process to address the intergenerational disadvantage many communities suffer. It will help overcome the historical exclusion of First Nations people from public forums. And crucially, it will offer an important symbolic gesture of acknowledgement and recognition that the days of *vox nullius* (voicelessness), the primary intention and consequence of *terra nullius*, are at last over.

It is, of course, unlikely that all First Nations people will speak with one voice – indeed, that would be undesirable. However, creation of a secure channel of communication will open up new ways for all members of the Australian community to negotiate their differences and discover novel solutions to our common challenges.

First Nations people will therefore not be the only ones to gain from the Voice. A vibrant, living platform for vigorous dialogue that addresses fundamental political issues will also benefit the wider society. It will help revive the ailing public sphere in Australia, restoring trust in institutions that have been degraded and depleted as a result of a deeply established focus on personal ambition, vested interests and loss of shared ethical vision.[3]

Linda Burney is a cabinet minister in the Albanese Government and the Minister for Indigenous Australians. She was previously a minister in the New South Wales Government and a member of the Council for Aboriginal Reconciliation. She is committed to grassroots community education about the Voice in preparation for the 2023 referendum. She spoke about the Voice at the 25th anniversary dinner for Australians for Native Title and Reconciliation (ANTAR). She said:

> The Voice means consulting with Aboriginal and Torres Strait Islander people about the matters that affect us. The Voice means delivering better practical outcomes. Practical outcomes in health, education and housing.
>
> The Voice is not to be a third chamber, nor will it have veto powers. As the Prime Minister has said, the Voice will be 'an unflinching source of advice and accountability. A body with the perspective and the power and the platform to tell the government and the parliament the truth about what is working and what is not.' The Voice will be consulted on matters directly affecting Aboriginal and Torres Strait Islander people – like Indigenous health, education and family violence.[4]

---

3   Pat Anderson et al, 'Why a First Nations Voice should come before Treaty', *The Conversation*, 22 October 2022, available at https://theconversation.com/why-a-first-nations-voice-should-come-before-treaty-192388

4   Linda Burney, 'Australians for Native Title and Reconciliation (ANTAR) 25th Anniversary Dinner', 12 October 2022 available at https://ministers.pmc.gov.au/burney/2022/australians-native-title-and-reconciliation-antar-25th-anniversary-dinner

She identified common principles for the Voice as a body that:

- provides independent advice to the Parliament and Government
- is chosen by First Nations people based on the wishes of local communities
- is representative of Aboriginal and Torres Strait Islander communities
- is empowering, community led, inclusive, respectful, culturally informed, gender balanced, and includes young people
- is accountable and transparent and
- works alongside existing organisations and traditional structures.

She was insistent that the Voice would not have a program delivery function and would not have a veto power.

She concluded:

For decades, Governments and bureaucrats in Canberra have thought they knew the solutions for our communities, better than the people actually living in our communities. We simply can't accept more of the same. More of the same poor outcomes. More of the same gaps in life expectancy. More of the same wasted opportunities. We can't accept that any longer. That is why the Voice to Parliament is needed. Because the Voice to Parliament will mean that governments of all persuasions will need to consult and listen to Aboriginal and Torres Strait Islander people on the issues that affect them.

And an Aboriginal and Torres Strait Islander Voice to Parliament will make Australia a better place for everyone. I think most Australians want to see First Nations people thrive and prosper like so many people that have come to these shores to make a home and raise a family.

Senator **Patrick Dodson** has been Director of the Central and Kimberley Land Councils. He served as a Commissioner in the Royal Commission into Aboriginal Deaths in Custody. He was the inaugural Chair of the Council for Aboriginal Reconciliation and Co-Chair of the 2012 Expert Panel for Constitutional Recognition of Indigenous Australians. He is now the Albanese Government's Special Envoy for Reconciliation and Implementation of the Uluru Statement. Addressing the Senate on 7 September 2022, he said:

As envisaged in the *Uluru Statement from the Heart*, the Voice to Parliament is a modest and generous invitation to the nation. Out of the torment of our powerlessness, it weaves a simple and hopeful suggestion for a way forward. It proposes a First Nations representative body to advise the parliament on the laws and policies that will impact upon their lives, and it proposes that this body, the Voice, be enshrined in the Constitution to ensure it has a place of recognition, responsibility and contribution into the future.

A Voice means that First Nations people, the people who know what works, will advise the parliament in a focused and consistent manner about laws that impact their lives. It is about shaping better policies and strategies that make a practical difference. It is about getting it right for the first time. It is about giving a constant voice to the people who don't have one. It is not the end of the road. It is not the only thing we need to do. But it is the next significant nation-building step in our journey towards reconciliation.[5]

He addressed the Senate again on 23 November 2022:

What First Nations people have asked for is a very simple thing: a say in how the parliament makes laws about their wellbeing and their lives. It will give Aboriginal and Torres Strait Islander peoples a say on the issues that affect them – after 250 years, not a bad idea – by allowing communities to have a say on their destinies, and that will improve their lives and their circumstances. The government's role is to ensure that the bricks and mortar of a referendum are sound and that we give the Australian people the best chance of making a clear and considered decision on a voice to parliament. We are consulting with First Nations leaders and constitutional experts to lay the groundwork for a referendum.

Let me share one part of the work to date, a set of principles for the Voice that have been agreed by the working group. It will be a body that provides independent advice to the parliament and the government. It will be chosen by Aboriginal and Torres Strait Islander peoples based on the wishes of their local communities. It will be representatives of those communities. It will be gender balanced and include youth. It will be accountable and transparent, and it will work alongside existing organisations and traditional

5   Senate, *Hansard*, 7 September 2022, p. 86.

structures. The Voice will not have a program delivery function. Nor will it have a veto over the parliament or the executive government.[6]

While many voters will be supportive of a Voice to Parliament providing Indigenous perspectives on any proposed special laws – specifically applicable to Indigenous Australians, their land rights and cultural heritage – some will be cautious about a Voice that can make representations not only to Parliament but also to executive government and in relation to any matters of concern to Indigenous Australians. Questions have been asked whether such an expanded Voice would risk litigation in the courts and needless clogging of the daily working of Government.

Retired High Court Judge **Kenneth Hayne** is chairing the Albanese Government's Constitutional Expert Group on the Voice. He was on the High Court when the judges made it clear that the Executive Government could not completely exclude the judges from reviewing decisions by Commonwealth public servants in relation to the asylum claims of non-citizens. Presumably he would have a fair sense of how the High Court would deal with a constitutional entity (the Voice) having a constitutional entitlement to make representations to public servants about all manner of things. If public servants were to treat such representations as junk mail in their in-boxes, presumably the High Court would intervene.

Hayne sought to address fears about ongoing litigation in relation to a Voice having a constitutional entitlement to make representations to Executive Government on any matters which

---

6   Senate, *Hansard*, 23 November 2022, p. 38.

the Voice members thought relevant to Indigenous Australians. He wrote:

If the voice makes a representation to the executive, I suppose someone may say that the executive did not consider what was said. Again, finding a plaintiff with standing to make that submission may be difficult. But get past that hurdle; if that person could show the executive had ignored what was said, the resulting decision could be undone only if the decision-maker was bound to have regard to what was said. And whether a decision-maker would be bound to take it into account would be a matter for debate. Assume, however, that the decision-maker were bound to consider what was said, isn't that the very point of the Voice – to give First Peoples a Voice in matters relating to First Peoples? And the most that could happen is that the decision-maker would be told to remake the decision. And in remaking the decision, what the Voice said would be one matter to take into account. It would not dictate the outcome. So I do not see future litigation derailing operation of the Voice.[7]

---

7   Kenneth Hayne, 'Fear of the voice lost in the lack of legal argument', *The Australian*, 28 November 2022, available at https://www.theaustralian.com.au/commentary/fear-of-the-voice-lost-in-the-lack-of-legal-argument/news-story/9696d03a566d3d946a74b7035175a 9e4

CHAPTER EIGHT
The 'No' Case

Senator **Jacinta Price** is a Country Liberal Party Senator for the Northern Territory. Having been deputy mayor of Alice Springs she is well familiar with the plight of remote Aboriginal communities. In her first speech to Parliament, she spoke of 'platitudes of motherhood statements from our now Labor Prime Minister who suggests without any evidence whatsoever that a Voice to Parliament bestowed upon us through the virtuous act of symbolic gesture by this government is what is going to empower us.'[1] She told the Senate:

> Prime Minister, we don't need another 'hand out' as you have described the 'Uluru Statement' to be. No, we Indigenous Australians have not come to agreement on this statement – as also what you have claimed. It would be far more dignifying if we were recognised and respected as individuals in our own right who are not simply defined by our racial heritage but by the content of our character.
>
> I am an empowered Warlpiri/Celtic Australian woman who did not, and has never needed, a paternalistic government to bestow my own empowerment upon me. We've proven for decades now that we do not need a Chief

---

1   Senate, *Hansard*, 27 July 2022 p, 120, also available at https://www.jacintaprice.com/maiden-speech

Protector of Aborigines. I have got here along with 10 other Indigenous voices, including my colleague Senator for South Australia Kerryn Liddle, within this 47th parliament of Australia like every other parliamentarian: through hard work and sheer determination.

However, now you want to ask the Australian people to disregard our elected voices and vote yes to apply a constitutionally enshrined advisory body without any detail of what that might in fact entail! Perhaps a word of advice – since that is what you're seeking: Listen to everyone and not just those who support your virtue-signalling agenda but also to those you contradict.[2]

Anthony Dillon is an academic and long-time commentator on Indigenous affairs. He writes regularly in *The Spectator*. He identifies as both Aboriginal and Australian. He believes that 'the current popular ideologies which portray Indigenous people merely as victims of history and White Australia (the invasion and racism) should be challenged'. In one of his earliest pieces opposing constitutional recognition of any sort, he wrote in 2014:

Recognition of culture in the Constitution has the potential to open the gate to different rules for people with Aboriginal ancestry and [it has] become a 'lawyer's picnic'. One very concerning example of different rules is the insistence on placing children in need of short-term and long-term care with 'culturally appropriate' carers. Currently, for children with Aboriginal ancestry (however minimal),

---

2   Ibid, pp. 120-121.

the Aboriginality of potential carers is given far too much weight. This practice has sometimes ended in tragedy. Some children have suffered, all in the name of 'culture'. A colour-blind culture or way of life, characterised by love is a far more important consideration than a culture that is assumed to be Aboriginal simply because the adult potential carers themselves have some Aboriginal ancestry.

Let us not forget the obvious elephant in the room – who is an Aborigine? Currently, anyone with any Aboriginal ancestry is entitled to identify as an Aboriginal Australian. This generous criterion is aligned with the ridiculous mantra, 'You are either Aboriginal or you are not.' Categorising Australians as Aboriginal, or not, by these rules contributes to the emergence of 'Aboriginal experts' who act as gatekeepers and significantly influence the national discussion on Aboriginal affairs. As a consequence of the stridency of these 'expert voices' (some of whom only discover their voices in the later stages of their lives), discussions are monitored and controlled to the point where non-Aboriginal people are constrained in expressing their opinions on matters that affect their fellow Australians. Some are not game to open their mouth because so many of these gatekeepers loudly proclaim that non-Aboriginal people have no right to have or to express an opinion on these matters. This 'us-vs-them' separatism lines the pockets of a few, but keeps many Aboriginal people from reaching their full potential.

My gravest concern is that recognising culture in the Constitution has the potential to accentuate the us-vs-them divide. Even more dangerously, privileging Aboriginal culture with the full force of the law has the potential to spark a 'feeding frenzy' of 'culture vultures', an endless welter of ever more strident demands for special consideration. Perhaps my concerns are unfounded, but I suggest that we need to think it through very carefully. We need to ask ourselves: will changing the Constitution put food on the table, get kids into school, adults into jobs, and families living in safe, clean environments?[3]

Warren Mundine is a successful businessman who has had a colourful political history, having been national president of the Labor Party, a member of Tony Abbott's Indigenous Affairs Council and an unsuccessful candidate for the Liberal Party in a federal election. He is Director of the Indigenous Forum at the conservative Centre for Independent Studies. He writes:

People ask me why I am opposed to the *Uluru Statement from the Heart* and an Aboriginal and Torres Strait Islander Voice to Parliament. It is a simple question, and I have a simple answer.

The assumption that Aboriginal and Torres Strait Islander people don't already have a voice to Parliament, or that Indigenous voices are limited, is ridiculous.

All my adult life there have been Aboriginal and Torres Strait Islander voices in Canberra. The Federal Council for the Advancement of Aborigines and Torres Strait Islanders

---

3   Anthony Dillon 'Recognition may mean never closing the gap', in Gary Johns, *Recognise What?* Connor Court, 2014, pp. 60-61.

(FCAATSI), the National Aboriginal Consultative Council (NACC), National Aboriginal Council (NAC), the Aboriginal Development Commission (ADC), the Aboriginal and Torres Strait Islander Commission (ATSIC), the National Congress of Australia's First Peoples, the Reconciliation Council, the National Indigenous Council, the Prime Minister's Indigenous Advisory Council, the Coalition of the Peaks, the Torres Strait Regional Authority, and the Torres Strait Regional Council, Northern Land Council, Central Land Council, the National Native Title Council and numerous other Land Councils and Peak Industry Bodies in Health, Education, Law, Justice, Children, etc.

And then we have had advisory committees to Ministers for Education, Health, and more. As well as individual Aboriginal and Torres Strait Islander people lobbying, Aboriginal and Torres Strait Islander members of various political parties and their Aboriginal and Torres Strait Islander policy committees. Not to mention festivals and conferences such as Garma and Barunga, which politicians, corporates and special interest groups attend.

I would argue the loudest voices are from individual Aboriginal and Torres Strait Islander people who communicate all the different viewpoints within our communities. And, yes, there is not one Aboriginal and Torres Strait Islander viewpoint. There are many – just like for the rest of Australia. If the vast array of councils, committees, coalitions and conferences over half a century haven't delivered the outcomes Indigenous people want to see, what makes anyone think a 'Voice to Parliament' will be any different simply because the power to create it sits in the Constitution?

I don't understand why it needs to be in the Constitution at all. And I haven't been convinced by any argument on this so far. The Constitution is the fundamental law underpinning our nation that all other laws must comply with. If it is to be amended or meddled with, then it should be for a bloody good reason — and it should be something that will make us a better and more united nation (as was the case for the 1967 referendum).

The Voice to Parliament will be nothing more than another huge bureaucracy to control Indigenous lives. The same old, same old.[4]

Writing in *The Australian*, Mundine says:

This new government must embrace a new mindset when considering how best to empower Aboriginal people to be all that they can be. However, with its focus on the *Uluru Statement from the Heart*, it is questionable as to whether such a mindset will be adopted. The principal focus of the statement, the Indigenous Voice to Parliament, seems to be a repackaging of the same old dogma that has defined (and failed) Aboriginal affairs for too many years; namely,

---

4   Nyunggai Warren Mundine, 'Push for a Voice to Parliament is a bureaucratic power grab to give Indigenous Australians rights they already have', Centre for Independent Studies, 9 August 2022, available at https://www.cis.org.au/commentary/opinion/push-for-a-voice-to-parliament-is-a-bureaucratic-power-grab-to-give-indigenous-australians-rights-they-already-have/

that only Aboriginal people are qualified to speak about Aboriginal issues.

We offer some ideas here that reflect a new mindset. These ideas will be unpopular with many, but they need to be, otherwise we will see only a repeat of what we've seen for the past few generations where symbolism, quotas, grand statements against racism and talkfests rule. This mindset will pave the way for a focus on jobs, education, housing, modern services and all the other benefits most other Australians take for granted. All this contributes greatly to long, rich lives, which, as Australian citizens, is the absolute right of Aboriginal Australians as Australian citizens.

A new mindset must challenge the myth that Aboriginal people are vastly different from other Australians. While there may be some minor differences between Aboriginal Australians and their non-Aboriginal brothers and sisters, they have the same needs and desires: to live in safe and clean environments, to have an education that equips them for the modern world, to have an opportunity to engage in service to their local and broader communities, and to have access to basic goods and services such as modern health facilities and fresh food. In far too many communities these basic rights are missing.

This belief that Aboriginal people are a different species requiring 'culturally appropriate' solutions has kept an Aboriginal industry thriving and allowed politicians, academics and consultants to build successful careers for themselves while people on the ground languish. Just look at how much attention this new government gives to the

Uluru statement – considerably more than what is being given to the dysfunction in remote communities.[5]

As prime minister, **Tony Abbott** was an advocate for completing the Constitution, not changing it. He was rightly renowned for his commitment to improving the lives of Aboriginal and Torres Strait Islander peoples on remote communities and committed himself to spending a week each year while prime minister with one of the remote communities. He has spent years in dialogue with Noel Pearson but remains unconvinced about the Voice. He wrote very forthrightly:

Recognising Indigenous people in the Constitution is well worth doing, but only if it's done in ways that don't damage our system of government and don't compromise our national unity. Done well, recognition would complete our Constitution rather than change it. Done badly, recognition would entrench race-based separatism and make the business of government even harder than it currently is.'

In my judgment, there are four massive issues with this concept of Indigenous recognition by way of a voice. First, it's a race-based body comprising only Indigenous people. Unless the government is to nominate or the parliament is to select the members of the Voice, there would presumably have to be a race-based electoral roll determining who could stand for election and who could vote for the

---

5   Nyunggai Warren Mundine, 'New mindset of action must replace grand symbolic gestures', *The Australian*, 20 July 2022, available at https://www.theaustralian.com.au/commentary/new-mindset-of-action-must-replace-grand-symbolic-gestures/news-story/23c66f4209b1c0bc5760e04c67d443fb

Voice's members. This would give Indigenous people two votes: first, like everyone else, a vote for the parliament itself; and second, in a right that's uniquely theirs, a vote for the Voice. If governments were in the habit of making decisions for Indigenous people without their input, or if the parliament were devoid of Indigenous representation, there might at least be an argument for such a special Indigenous body. As it's happened though, constitutionally entrenching a separate Indigenous voice when there are already 11 individual Indigenous voices in the parliament, and when there's arguably 'analysis paralysis' from a surfeit of Indigenous consultation mechanisms already, is a pretty strange way to eliminate racism from our Constitution and from our institutional arrangements.

Second, it would vastly complicate the difficulties of getting legislation passed and anything done. If the Voice chooses to have a view on anything at all that touches Indigenous people, that view would have to be taken very seriously by government; indeed, as the PM has admitted, it would be a veto, in fact, if not in theory.

Third, in the event that an Indigenous person or entity were aggrieved by a government that failed to give the Voice a chance to make representations on any issue, or that then ignored it, there could readily be an application to the High Court to rule that the Constitution had been breached. This is the likely consequence of importing into the Constitution such a vague-yet-portentous concept as a 'Voice' (as opposed to one described as an advisory body or a commission), especially one that's said to be the means of putting an end to centuries of marginalisation. At the very least, the existence of a Voice could import further delay into the finalisation of legislation or decision-making as it's given adequate time to investigate and come to its conclusions.

Fourth, the whole point of Indigenous recognition is to address a gap in what's otherwise been an admirable Constitution and, in so doing, to help to complete the reconciliation of Indigenous people with modern Australia. There could hardly be a greater setback to reconciliation than a referendum that fails. Yet that is the likelihood – at least based on the record of previous attempts to change the Constitution – in the absence of substantial bipartisan support. Although the Coalition's Indigenous affairs spokesperson has previously been an in-principle supporter of a Voice, the new Coalition senator for the Northern Territory, the proud 'Celtic Warlpiri Australian' woman Jacinta Price, has expressed deep scepticism about a proposal with so much of the detail thus far omitted, with so much potential for ineffective posturing, and that defines people by racial heritage.

I can understand why many Indigenous leaders would want constitutional change to go beyond the symbolic in order to produce better outcomes for their own people, and hence the call for their own unique voice to which the parliament should defer. But better outcomes are ultimately the product of better attitudes, and these are more likely to be engendered by a generous acknowledgment of all the elements that have made modern Australia such a special place than by creating yet more elements of government based on Indigenous ancestry.

Based on what we currently know, the Voice is wrong in principle, almost sure to be bad in practice, and unlikely to succeed in any referendum. If it fails, reconciliation is set back. If it succeeds, our country is permanently divided by race. Hence the fundamental question: why further consider something that would leave us worse off whichever way it goes?[6]

Ian Callinan served on the High Court with Kenneth Hayne. He is a well-known constitutional conservative, having been placed on the High Court by John Howard when Tim Fischer at the time of the *Wik* decision was calling for a 'capital C conservative' to be placed on the court. Callinan disagreed with Hayne's assurance that there was nothing to fear from the Voice. In particular, he thought Hayne was underplaying the prospect of litigation that might arise were a Voice to executive government, as well as to parliament, to be placed in the Constitution. He said that 'like senator Jacinta Nampijinpa Price and many other Australians, including many, many lawyers of goodwill, I do not think the Voice is the way'. He wrote cordially and respectfully but very firmly:

Stretching my imagination only a little, I would foresee a decade or more of constitutional and administrative law litigation arising out of a Voice whether constitutionally

---

6   Tony Abbott, 'Pass or fail, this referendum will surely leave us worse off', *The Australian*, 5 November 2022, available at https://www.theaustralian.com.au/inquirer/pass-or-fail-this-referendum-will-surely-leave-us-worse-off/news-story/761616d76aaa8e5e308ed9ce1d04c 8ba

entrenched or not. Every state and territory are likely to have an interest in any representations and in the interactions between the Voice and the constitutionally entrenched houses of parliament and executive government.

It is one thing to say the Voice can make representations only, but in the real world of public affairs, as the Prime Minister candidly acknowledged, it would be a brave parliament that failed to give effect to representations of the Voice.

Who knows what a future High Court might do as it seeks to juggle the respective rights, obligations and 'expectations' to which the voice would give rise? I can imagine any number of people and legal personalities in addition to the states who might plausibly argue that they have standing.

Standing is a highly contestable matter. It is an opaque and plastic concept. Whether a person has standing or not is itself a justiciable question of the kind regularly heard and determined by the courts, expansively so in recent times. One has only to glance at the litigation that environmental concerns have generated as to standing to see that this is so.

I have no doubt that already, courageous and ingenious legal minds both are conceiving bases upon which to litigate the many legal and cultural implications of the Voice. The Voice, or a member of it, is almost certain to argue in the courts that a member of the executive government, in executing a parliamentary enactment of a representation of the Voice, took into account an irrelevant consideration, or

106

failed to take into account a relevant one, or made a decision that no reasonable person could make, shifting [indicators] relied upon in almost every challenge brought to the actions of government.[7]

---

7   Ian Callinan, 'Examining the case for the voice – an argument against', *The Australian*, 17 December 2022, available at https://www.theaustralian.com.au/inquirer/examining-the-case-for-the-voice-an-argument-against/news-story/e30c8f2ffcbae73eaa3921e82bf174a9

CHAPTER NINE
Where to from here?

It's now eight years since Aboriginal and Torres Strait Islander Delegates took all options for constitutional recognition, other than the Voice, off the table. As Amanda Vanstone put it when on the Referendum Council, there is now only one shot in the locker. There is no getting around Vanstone's observation: 'Whilst one would expect that Australians would not support something which Indigenous Australia did not endorse it is not clear that they would automatically endorse whatever Indigenous Australia prefers.' The task today is the same as it was when the Referendum Council completed its work in 2017. As Vanstone put it: 'The task therefore is to find a version of an Indigenous voice to parliament that will be acceptable to Indigenous Australians and the parliament of the day.'

There is no point in the Albanese government claiming that all the necessary detail about the Voice is to be found in the Langton-Calma Report. Having been a member of that Senior Advisory Group, I can attest that we complied with our government remit. There were two matters specified as being out of scope for us:

(a) final decision on which options progress to testing
(b) making recommendations as a Group through this co-design process on constitutional recognition, including

determining the referendum question or when a referendum should be held.[1]

We are yet to finalise the words to be placed in the Constitution constituting the Voice. To date, the government and its various consultative groups have been unilaterally tinkering with just one of 18 suggestions which were put to the joint parliamentary committee in 2018, this one having been submitted nearly two months after the closing date for submissions, and just 26 days before the committee was required to submit its final report.

Linda Burney has adopted Noel Pearson's metaphor that this referendum be viewed as the government effectively asking, 'Do we need a bridge to cross the Sydney harbour: yes or no'? That metaphor would be fine if the government was proposing only what the Referendum Council had recommended, namely a representative body giving Aboriginal and Torres Strait Islander peoples a Voice to the Parliament a Voice to the Parliament. But Anthony Albanese was asking Australians to build an altogether different bridge when he added to the second sentence of his Garma formula that representations could also be made to 'the Executive government on matters relating to Aboriginal and Torres Strait Islander Peoples'.[2]

This is a bridge too far for many respected political commentators such as Paul Kelly who has pointed out that this second sentence:

---

1   Indigenous Co-Design Process, *Final Report to the Australian Government*, July 2021, p. 240.
2   Paul Karp, 'Claims Labor lacks detail on Indigenous voice are 'rubbish', Linda Burney tells Woodford folk festival', *The Guardian*, 28 December 2022, available at https://www. theguardian.com/australia-news/2022/dec/28/claims-labor-lacks-detail-on-indigenous-voice-are-rubbish-linda-burney-tells-woodford-folk-festival

… is open-ended, unqualified and unlimited. It means the Voice can make representations to the parliament on bills, to the executive government on ministerial decisions, but is not limited to matters before the government or parliament. The Voice can make representations on virtually anything or even initiate its own agendas. Given this provision, it will be a brave and probably foolhardy parliament that tries to restrict the Voice acting under the third sentence in Albanese's constitutional provision where the parliament can make laws with respect to the 'composition, functions, powers and procedures' of the Voice.[3]

Clearly there is a need for greater precision in the suggested wording of any constitutional amendment. When being interviewed by Katharine Murphy in 2022, the Prime Minister said:

What I'm trying to do is to lead by advancing what a question and a constitutional amendment would look like without being too prescriptive – to give people space, so this isn't my proposal. I want this to be Australia's proposal going forward.[4]

Speaking to the media after his appearance at the 2022 Woodford Folk Festival at Christmas time, the Prime Minister said, 'It has now been more than four months since that was put

3   Paul Kelly, 'Conviction not enough for PM on the voice', *The Australian*, 3 August 2022 available at https://www.theaustralian.com.au/commentary/conviction-not-enough-for-pm-on-the-voice/news-story/46431a2cecd2eb58440168588c85a1ca
4   K. Murphy, 'Lone Wolf: Albanese and the New Politics' in *Quarterly Essay*, QE 88, November 2022, pp.96–7.

out there for consultation. We will continue to engage in the lead-up to the referendum.'[5]

On 9 January 2023, the Prime Minister was even more open to suggested amendments when he told the ABC's *7.30* program:

This isn't my proposal. This is the people's proposal. And I very consciously in that Garma speech didn't say, 'Here's the words. This is the Government's position.' I said, 'Here is draft words. If you have a better idea, then I'm certainly open to ways in which, if people think that improvements can be made then by all means, come forward with them.'[6]

On 18 January 2023, the Prime Minister went on the front foot inviting suggested changes to the Garma wording when he told Ben Fordham on Sydney radio 2GB:

There will be a process whereby people can make submissions to the parliamentary inquiry, which will be about the words that will go forward in the referendum. And that will be a process whereby Australians can all put forward their views and suggestions about the wording that is going forward... The elected Parliament will determine the words going forward. This is not my proposal. This isn't the Government's proposal. This needs to be the people's proposal.[7]

5   Anthony Albanese, *ABC News Breakfast, Transcript*, 29 December 2022 available at https://www.pm.gov.au/media/abc-news-breakfast
6   ABC *7.30*, 9 January 2023, available at https://www.pm.gov.au/media/television-interview-abc-730-1
7   Anthony Albanese, Interview, Radio 2GB with Ben Fordham, 18 January 2023, available at https://www.pm.gov.au/media/radio-interview-2gb-ben-fordham-live

Taking up this express invitation to all citizens to participate at this stage of the process, I suggest a simplified amendment to provide: 'There shall be an Aboriginal and Torres Strait Islander Voice with such structure and functions as the Parliament deems necessary to facilitate consultation prior to the making of special laws with respect to Aboriginal and Torres Strait Islander peoples, and with such other functions as the Parliament determines.'[8]

This would be a way of completing the Constitution, not changing it, and consistent with the *Uluru Statement*.

The Voice could be given additional functions by legislation. Those additional functions could include representations to Parliament on laws other than special laws with respect to Aboriginal and Torres Strait Islander peoples, as well as representations to government on laws and policies impacting on Aboriginal and Torres Strait Islander peoples. But these would not be constitutional functions of the Voice. The Voice's structure would be determined by legislation and could be varied from time to time by legislation.

For a national Voice to have utility, credibility and legitimacy, it needs to be resourced with a comprehensive system of local and regional ears which can listen to the local and regional voices. A national Voice without numerous ears and the means for transmitting local and regional voices to the national stage would be a clashing cymbal, or, as Noel Pearson once described the proposed Congress of Australia's First Peoples, 'a blackfella's wailing wall', a

---

8   I first proposed a suggestion along these lines in a letter to *The Australian*, 27 January 2022 See https://www.theaustralian.com.au/commentary/letters/most-australians-are-tolerant-and-inclusive-so-stop-the-hectoring-on-our-national-day/news-story/5df6d8d9cce30994 761c822899f19281

forum for victimhood.[9] A Voice with ears could be the ideal body to complete the Constitution so that special laws applying only to the First Australians and their heritage would be enacted only after due consultation with them.

This is not the stuff of wedges; it's the glue to consolidate the unity of the Australian polity in the twenty-first century. I would hope that Tony Abbott and Jacinta Price could approve such a measure. This is the absolute minimum of what a constitutional Voice to Parliament should include. The question will be whether it is sufficient to satisfy the advocates from Uluru. In the end, there will be little point in proceeding with a referendum unless the words for insertion in the Constitution win the support of Noel Pearson as well as the likes of John Howard.

The Parliament now needs to provide a process for all persons of good will to submit their suggested wording. Thus Parliament might find that cherished common ground, agreeing on 'the specific content, wording and timing of a referendum proposal',[10] enhancing the prospects of winning the support of the majority of voters in the majority of states. In this urgent and important search, I offer my suggested wording of the constitutional amendment for the scrutiny of constitutional lawyers, Indigenous leaders and all participants in the public square.

In 1967, the Australian people voted overwhelmingly for a change to the Constitution which was minimal and symbolic. It was

---

9   Debra Jopson, 'New indigenous "company" structured to keep politicians at arm's length', *Sydney Morning Herald*, 3 May 2010 at https://www.smh.com.au/national/new-indigenous-company-structured-to-keep-politicians-at-arms-length-20100502-u1hx.html

10   Joint Select Committee on Constitutional Recognition of Aboriginal and Torres Strait Islander Peoples, *Progress Report*, June 2013, para. 3.19.

the popular vote which provided the momentum for real, substantive policy change. We moved from *terra nullius* to land rights, from assimilation to self-determination. This time, with another largely symbolic change to the Constitution approved overwhelmingly by the voters, we could move from the First Australians being counted to the First Australians being heard when laws and policies are made affecting them. This proposed amendment could provide constitutional recognition of First Australians through constitutional recognition of a Voice which parliament can reshape from time to time, ensuring that the workings of government are not clogged and that the courts are not constantly involved in reviewing relations between the Voice and government.

We should go to referendum only if one of the following three conditions is fulfilled:

1. The proposed change to the Constitution should be an accurate reflection of the recommendation made by the Referendum Council and as interpreted by Murray Gleeson – a member of that Council and retired Chief Justice, who spoke of a *Voice to Parliament* and not of a *Voice to Parliament* and *executive government*.

2. Failing that condition, if the proposed change is to go beyond that, it should be approved by the Parliament after consideration of a published legal opinion provided by the Solicitor General.

3. Failing that condition, if the wording is not to be subject to some parliamentary process, the government should be completely transparent and inform the public about the process followed to adopt the wording and

the reasons for such wording. The government should publish competent legal advice assuring voters that the constitutional change will not risk ongoing judicial review of administrative decisions likely to clog the working of good government.

Bob Ellicott, as Attorney-General in 1977, was the proponent for three of Australia's eight successful referendums. It was his view that 'for a referendum proposal to have a substantial chance of acceptance', it 'should contain no element of possible substantial confusion on legal or other grounds'.[11]

A Voice to Parliament, in relation to laws enacted especially to apply to Aboriginal and Torres Strait Islander peoples, is the necessary minimum requirement for constitutional recognition in the 21st century. As Murray Gleeson has said:

It is difficult to see any objection in principle to the creation of a body to advise Parliament about proposed laws relating to Indigenous affairs, and specifically about special laws enacted under the race power which, in its practical operation, is now a power to make laws about Indigenous people.[12]

---

11   R. Ellicott, 'Indigenous Recognition: Some Issues' in *Proceedings of the Twenty-Third Conference of The Samuel Griffith Society*, 2012, p. 80.

12   Murray Gleeson, *Recognition in keeping with the Constitution: A worthwhile project*, Uphold and Recognise, PM Glynn Institute, Australian Catholic University, 2019, p. 12. Noel Pearson has said: 'Mr Gleeson's speech is the last word on the legal integrity of the Voice and its seamless compatibility with the constitutional history of the Australian Commonwealth.' (Noel Pearson, *Address to Garma Festival*, 3 August 2019, available at https://capeyorkpartnership.org.au/all-we-seek-is-our-rightful-place-thank-you/)

Those politicians in our Parliament opposed to a Voice with such a defined constitutional purpose need to be able to answer Gleeson's question:

How does it offend some principle of equality now to provide that, in recognition of the unique position of Indigenous people in the nation's history, Parliament shall establish a representative body which has a particular function of giving advice about such laws?[13]

Equality in 21st century Australia demands such formal constitutional recognition.

Should the government fail to reach agreement in the Parliament on the proposed new wording for the Constitution, I think it would be for the best if the referendum were postponed until a new generation of national leaders can come to the table, putting right what was left unresolved, by seeking agreement between our Indigenous and parliamentary leaders.

Now is the time for increased community engagement and education on this issue so that all Australians can contribute to national understanding and agreement. Regardless of whether or not constitutional recognition is achieved during this parliamentary term, the government will still be able to legislate for a Voice. However, I maintain hope that agreement can be reached in our present Parliament, and we can get to 'Yes' on the Voice when we all go into the ballot box later this year answering the simple, clear question: 'Do you support an alteration to the Constitution that establishes an Aboriginal and Torres Strait Islander Voice?' It's time

---

13   Ibid, p. 15.

for constitutional recognition of the First Australians on terms acceptable to them and the nation.

APPENDIX
Uluru Statement From The Heart

We, gathered at the 2017 National Constitutional Convention, coming from all points of the southern sky, make this statement from the heart:

Our Aboriginal and Torres Strait Islander tribes were the first sovereign Nations of the Australian continent and its adjacent islands, and possessed it under our own laws and customs. This our ancestors did, according to the reckoning of our culture, from the Creation, according to the common law from 'time immemorial', and according to science more than 60,000 years ago.

This sovereignty is *a spiritual notion: the ancestral tie between the land, or 'mother nature', and the Aboriginal and Torres Strait Islander peoples who were born therefrom, remain attached thereto, and must one day return thither to be united with our ancestors. This link is the basis of the ownership of the soil, or better, of sovereignty.* It has never been ceded or extinguished, and co-exists with the sovereignty of the Crown.

How could it be otherwise? That peoples possessed a land for sixty millennia and this sacred link disappears from world history in merely the last two hundred years?

With substantive constitutional change and structural reform, we believe this ancient sovereignty can shine through as a fuller expression of Australia's nationhood.

Proportionally, we are the most incarcerated people on the planet. We are not an innately criminal people. Our children are aliened from their families at unprecedented rates. This cannot be because we have no love for them. And our youth languish in detention in obscene numbers. They should be our hope for the future.

These dimensions of our crisis tell plainly the structural nature of our problem. This is *the torment of our powerlessness.*

We seek constitutional reforms to empower our people and take *a rightful place* in our own country. When we have power over our destiny our children will flourish. They will walk in two worlds and their culture will be a gift to their country.

We call for the establishment of a First Nations Voice enshrined in the Constitution.

Makarrata is the culmination of our agenda: *the coming together after a struggle.* It captures our aspirations for a fair and truthful relationship with the people of Australia and a better future for our children based on justice and self-determination.

We seek a Makarrata Commission to supervise a process of agreement-making between governments and First Nations and truth-telling about our history.

In 1967 we were counted, in 2017 we seek to be heard. We leave base camp and start our trek across this vast country. We invite you to walk with us in a movement of the Australian people for a better future.

.

Fr Frank Brennan SJ is a Catholic priest and human rights lawyer. He was a member of the Langton-Calma committee on the co-design of the Indigenous Voice. In 2015, he published No Small Change: The Road to Recognition for Indigenous Australia. *Since then, he has been following closely every turn on that difficult road. During 2023, he will be speaking in parishes and schools in the lead-up to the forthcoming referendum on the Voice. He can be contacted at rector@newman.unimelb.edu.au. He is happy to assist any local groups wanting to enhance their understanding of Indigenous constitutional recognition.*

www.ingramcontent.com/pod-product-compliance
Lightning Source LLC
Chambersburg PA
CBHW052021030426
42335CB00026B/3246